The People Who Run: Being The Tragedy Of The Refugees In Russia

Violetta Thurstan

The People Who Run

Being
The Tragedy of the Refugees
in Russia

By

Violetta Thurstan
Author of " Field Hospital and Flying Column "

" *The greatest tragedy of the war is not seen
upon the battlefield* "

London and New York
G. P. Putnam's Sons
1916

First Published, June 1916

TO
LADY HENRY SOMERSET
WITH MY LOVE

Foreword

I HAVE many friends to thank; for without their kind offices these sketches of the refugees of many nations who have taken sanctuary in Russia could never have been written:

To the *President of the Tatiana Committee*, whose letter of recommendation proved such an Open Sesame all through Russia;

To *E. Birse, Esq.*, and *Monsieur Gregorieff, of Moscow*, who gave up so much of their precious time to show me what I most wanted to see;

To *Miss A. Bucknall*, not only for her unwearying devotion in interpreting for me and translating all kinds of tedious reports and documents, but also for accompanying me on a difficult journey into the interior of Russia in the depth of winter;

Foreword

To the *Professors and Students of Kazan University*, who gave me the truest impression of the real spirit of comradeship that I have ever received ;

to these and many more friends who gave me the beautiful Russian hospitality, and who took so much trouble to collect information, statistics, and photographs, I can only offer in return my very grateful thanks for all their kindness.

V. T.

May 1916.

viii

Contents

I

BÉJENTZE

THE Russian word for refugees is Béjentze. The word means "the people who run," and it would be difficult to find a more appropriate title for those five and a half million dazed and terrified people who fled away from their homes in the summer and autumn of 1915, before the great German advance into Russia.

From the farms and homesteads of Poland, the peaceful plains of Lithuania, the seaports of the Baltic provinces, from the mountains of Galicia and Ruthenia they fled, to escape the roaring cannon and the devastating fire of the enemy.

Their new home in the interior of Russia was to them a foreign country, where the language, religion, and customs differed very much from their own ; but their exile was made as little painful as possible by the kindness of the Russian peasants. Pity is one of the most marked and most beautiful characteristics of the Russian people. One may see the Russian soldier at the front giving not only his money and his food, but even his coat to a prisoner who looks ill and miserable. In this country a convicted criminal is almost always pitied rather than blamed. Even when a batch of prisoners from the front is marched through a town, you will hear more murmurs of commiseration than cheers of triumph from the watching crowd. So the whole generous heart of the people went out to these fugitives in their terrible distress during the great retreat into the interior. The sympathy and compassion were there ; alas, that there was no organization ready also to cope with the awful need !

In England we have seen and heard much at first hand of the misery of the Belgian refugees and know from personal experience how bravely it was borne. But much less is known of the sufferings of the refugees in Russia, chiefly because Russia is so far away and Russian news very scanty, and we as a nation find it difficult to visualize what we do not see and to realize what is happening in other countries without being told. Indeed,

2

Béjentze

no one who does not know Russia can imagine the immensity of the great empty distances, the absence of roads and railways, and the difficulty of transport even in times of peace ; much less can they fathom the depth of misery that this hurried flight entailed on " the people who run." Bitter as the sufferings of the Belgian refugees were, their *physical* privations were as nothing in comparison with what these people on the eastern frontiers have been called upon to endure. The mental and moral sufferings are, of course, common to both nations. Belgians and Poles alike have had to bear the loss of country, home, friends, money, in fact all that makes life most worth living to them, coming as strangers and pilgrims into a strange land, dependent for their very existence on the charity of others. But Poland's spiritual tragedy began a century and a half ago, when her nation was split up and her kingdom given to others. Now Pole is fighting against Pole, who are brothers, with the same nationality, language, religion, and. traditions. Belgium, again, is a little country densely populated and in easy communication with Holland, France, and England; the exodus there began in the summer and was

3

certainly over before the cold weather began. Russia, on the contrary, is an enormous country where the distances between towns are very great and where the climate is very severe.

The retreat had to be carried out very swiftly, under unheard-of difficulties, and here there were no convenient neutral countries close at hand to take off some of the refugees. The whole refugee problem was and is on an enormous scale, and it is very much to the credit of the Russian authorities that with so little machinery available at first, they were able to accomplish so much. For it was no mean feat to evacuate in such a short time whole villages, towns, provinces, countries even, and get the inhabitants removed from the danger zone, where every available transport of any kind was crowded already almost beyond its utmost capacity with retreating troops, fighting as they retired, and hampered with the ammunition and supplies of all kinds that must accompany them. The Russian journalist Kasiunine, writing in the *Novoe Vremya* on October 16, 1914, describes the scenes he witnessed in the refugee trains as a " terrific nightmare." It was a night-

4

mare, alas, from which they woke up to find it was true !

Verily the English language lacks words to express the suffering that these people underwent, and nothing that we can imagine could be worse than the reality.

The following sketches of the refugees are the result of a personal visit to Russia to inquire into the conditions under which they are living, and an attempt has been made to describe as briefly as possible what has been done for them already and what still wants doing. The difficulty has been, not to gather the material, but to sift from the great mass of reports, statistics. and facts, what seems to be most worth the telling.

The refugee problem will not by any means be over with the end of the war. The question of how it is going to be made possible for these poor souls to return to their devastated, ruined homes will then be a very difficult one to answer. In trying to find a solution of the difficulty, it must be remembered that it is not easy to help the people to help themselves. The iron has now entered into their souls. Many of them have lost so much that they have lost even hope, and they sit there

5

apathetically, with their hands in their laps, waiting for everything to be done for them. Their self-respect has been lowered by the overcrowding, lack of privacy, and the indiscriminate mingling of the decent and the dissolute. Their physical constitution has been injured by the privations of the long retreat, the scanty food, and the unhygienic conditions of their present surroundings. It is a curious fact that the worse their condition is, the less they have any desire to improve it. Many refugees prefer, indeed, to exist miserably in idleness on the twenty kopecks a day allowed by the Government rather than do even well-paid work.

A typical story illustrating this strange inertia was told me by a keen worker among the refugees. There was one very bad *barak* where refugees were housed, in a small country town in the interior of Russia. They were dreadfully overcrowded in this reeking, damp, dark house, deprived of the smallest decencies of life, and the children were dying at an alarming rate. A lady living in the town, deeply touched by their distress, offered a certain amount of milk every day for the children. For the first few days it was eagerly

6

fetched from her house, then intermittently, and finally no one troubled to come for it at all, so the offer was withdrawn. They had fallen into the abyss of dark despair, and had no wish to escape from it. There comes a time when it is less trouble to die than to live, and many of the refugees have reached this stage. This inertia which so many refugees suffer from has now been recognized as a definite medical lesion brought on by their privations, and must be distinguished from both slacking and shamming, which are also fairly common. Some of the local committees, notably in Kiev, have been very successful in treating this inertia, slowly but surely building up their shattered self-respect by finding them occupation and a fresh interest in life.

The most urgent of the many problems connected with the refugees is how to avert the terrible infant mortality among them. Even before the war, the percentage of infant mortality in Russia reached an abnormally high level in comparison with the rest of Europe ; now it has reached terrific proportions. The babies are dying like flies at the present moment, and just as at the front there are many more men wounded in proportion to those killed, so for each baby who dies there are a still larger number stunted, crippled, and injured for life, owing to their unhygienic surroundings. The adults—even the old people in some cases—have stood their privations very well, but the babies have a very slight hold on life ; they soon tire of the unkind world they have come into, and float back to Paradise without a single regret on their part for the smelly, noisy baraks and tenements they have left behind.

There is much work in this direction waiting to be done by some one. The future generation of citizens must somehow be saved, and England will surely not close her ears to this piteous cry for help. At least our country is not invaded, our villages laid waste, our people fugitives, our babies dying of want. The last Report from the Great Britain to Poland Fund states : " The more our [British] Fund can do, by so much the more can Russian energy and Russian brains be liberated to prosecute the unique object of the Allied nations, the crushing of our common enemy. Therefore every additional sovereign given to the Fund means the release of

8

another fraction of this pressure exerted on our heroic Ally, a pressure from the horror and weight of which the British Isles are, fortunately, spared." The Poles, who form a large proportion of the number of refugees, have a great claim on English sympathy, as Great Britain and Poland have long been knit by special ties and share national ideals and aspirations. Large sums towards the relief of the Polish fugitives have been already contributed by England. Each nationality has its own special claim and there are many funds, and every one can help the one that appeals to them most. But money is not enough. It is not only food, money, stores, clothing that are required, though God knows they are sorely needed enough ; above all, there is needed here personal service, so that these poor souls can be built up again, given back their earlier ideals, encouraged to work, and restored to their former self-respect. Then, when their star rises again in the horizon and the time comes for them to return to the country they love so well, they may be enabled to start again physically and mentally fit, taking up their new life vigorously, courageously, hopefully, forgetting

9

the dark past and looking forward with new hope into the dawning future. For the body of Poland has been sorely wounded by the enemy, but they can never kill her soul.

II

A JOURNEY TO RUSSIA

"We must look at the pilgrims on the road, discover if we can the motive of their travel, the maps which they use, the luggage which they take, the end which they attain."

E. UNDERHILL

ROMANCE is a rare and almost a despised quality in our materialistic world. But there are those for whom it is the breath of life, and they will know where to look for it, for it does still exist in certain places in spite of " organization," " standardization," " co-opertion," and other estimable and modern methods which, if we are not careful, are apt to smother and kill it. And the soil in which this rare plant flourishes is almost always to be found in those countries—such as Russia, Spain, Ireland—which have a curious instinct for suffering and a supreme indifference to the necessities of life. It is often associated with poverty, because, as St. Francis of Assisi

11

discovered for us long ago when he became
betrothed to Lady Poverty, we are then not
" entangled by temporal comforts " but are
free in spirit. Romance flourishes best where
there is a suggestion of infinity, of something
that cannot be encompassed or measured. In
Russia this sense of infinity is found in the
limitless rolling plains, or in the dark silence
of the icy tundras ; in Spain, in the naked
grimness of her austere mountain-peaks and
the wide horizons of her ochre-coloured table-
lands. A recent novelist well expressed the
romance of Ireland : " There is no other land
where the hand of the Maker is more poignantly
felt and where the mystic spirit of creation
has been so strangely preserved." In our own
noisy and crowded country Romance lingers
nowhere with more tenacity than in affairs
pertaining to the sea : partly, I suppose,
because of our primitive instinct for the sea,
which is almost a seventh sense with islanders ;
partly because that wilful lady entirely refuses
to be organized, would not co-operate with
any one in the world if she could help it, and
certainly possesses no standard of any kind,
so that Romance, who is as wayward and
unaccountable as the sea herself, tints sea-

12

faring matters with her glowing brush till
the mere mention of one of the old-fashioned
words or phrases will conjure up to the mind
a whole series of vividly coloured pictures.
Such a word, for instance, as " Wharf." The
very word sparkles with brine and calls up
memories of hardy mariners who set sail
thence for unknown seas. I never hear of a
wharf without its bringing back a whiff of
childhood when I thought that Longfellow
was the Greatest Poet in the World. I can
see now the green broken-backed volume in
which I used to read about

> "The black wharves and the ships,
> And the sea-tides tossing free,
> And Spanish sailors with bearded lips,
> And the beauty and majesty of the ships
> And the magic of the sea."

I remember quite vividly sitting in a big
fig-tree at the bottom of the garden reading
this, tasting each word separately and smack-
ing my lips over it. Certainly for any one
setting out to Russia, where Romance is
stored up in great heaps for any one who likes
to take away in both hands, it seems only
fitting that the start should be made from a
wharf, and not from a mere pier or landing-
stage.

The People Who Run

But I will say at the outset that the Norway Wharf, Newcastle, is essentially not a place for decrepit or aged folk. This was dark and deserted on the wild December night when we started for Russia, a north-westerly gale was shrieking down the river, dispersing the swirls of white mist that almost blotted out the few river lights, and an angry scud of rain stung our cheeks as we battled with the tempest. This, then, was the Norway Wharf. For a minute or two one could see nothing at all, and then we just discerned the outline of a little ship in front of us, her funnel and rigging standing out black, even against the blackness of the night. We stumbled down a high gangway as steep as a cliff, down again into the very depths of the ship, and arrived at the little cabin that was to be our home for the next forty-eight hours.

That screaming gale gave us awful warning of what was to come. More than one vessel setting out with us that night never reached her destination but perished in the wild North Sea, but our gallant little *Irma* buffeted her way through tremendous seas, shuddering and quivering as she breasted every spumy wave, straining at her leash until every board

14

groaned and started, rolling till she shipped great green rollers, now right, now left, righting herself every now and then with a horrible internal spasm, holding us as an angry mother in her clutch and shaking us till we were dizzy, yet never leaving go for a moment till she had us safe alongside the Bergen quay.

Here all was peace. Gay, friendly little sledges were awaiting the steamer, and galloped off with us to the hotel. The shops were still mostly open, though it was after nine o'clock at night, and the streets seemed brilliant in comparison with the sombre ones we had left behind in London. After the close atmosphere of the steamer the air tasted like iced champagne, and every frost-crystal seemed to sparkle and wink a welcome at us in the starlight as we flew over the creaking snow.

Suddenly a dead weight seemed to slip from our shoulders, and it was some time before I realized what had happened. We were now in a country where there was no war. In England and the other belligerent countries the strain of the war enshrouds one so evenly all round, like a fog at sea, that until it is suddenly lifted for a moment one hardly knows how heavily it has pressed.

Certainly the neutral countries have their own perplexities and difficulties, and the enthralling fear lest they too might reach the parting of the ways, but for them it is a horrible dream, not a reality. Here in Norway there were laughing, careless people who had no one at the front, who could live a whole day without looking at the newspapers, who could greet their friends cheerfully, even daring to ask after the absent ones without the quick sidelong glance first to see if it was safe to do so. A few days in a neutral country is a mental and physical rest, but one could not bear it long. One values too much the privilege of being allowed to be a performer in ever such a small part in the great drama that is being played, with the world for its stage, to share in the great struggle for liberty and future peace—above all, to have the chance, perhaps, of lifting a tiny corner of the veil of misery that hangs over those who have lost all that makes life most worth living.

War has revealed an entirely new conception of things to us. It is life now that is

16

lonely for so many, not death. Death no longer can be lonely for those on the other side of the river. One must almost imagine that life over there is merrier and lustier than usual, now that so many cheerful souls have met again after such a short interval. It must be like meeting as usual after the school holidays for those comrades who have lived their short years together, fought together for the team as it were, and died for a common goal.

We shall never grudge all it has cost, the blood and treasure that has been poured out, the loneliness of the fatherless and brotherless and widow, the sufferings of the refugees and the homeless, if only these supreme sacrifices have not been offered in vain. War is almost the most hideous thing in the world, but there are just a few worse catastrophes ; exploiting, cheating, grinding, money-grubbing are worse. We who are fighting in defence of the liberty of others will surely never return to the bad old days before the war when these rotten slaveries ate away our strength from underneath.

When the war ends, and we can again see clearly the great issues before us, then surely

B   17

this time we shall choose wider freedom, higher ideals, cleaner living. The habits of self-denial, even though perhaps learnt compulsorily, will have given us a clearer vision of what England's great destiny might be if we would.

First, we must strip ourselves bare of the last vestiges of the old snobbery, greed, humbug, jealousy; and then, purified by suffering, strengthened by self-denial, fortified by friendship and better understanding of the great nations who have allied themselves with us, it might be England's destiny to make a new world, to recapture the spirit of creation, the spirit of joy and of generous youth, which will enable us to reconstruct a real civilization bringing peace and goodwill that will endure for all time.

* * * *

We left Bergen in the cold winter dawn, and as the train crossed the steep mountain-range that divides Bergen from Christiania, painfully panting up some three thousand feet and then tearing down the other side as fast as possible, we watched the woolly grey clouds beginning to mass up until at last they

18

blotted out the horizon, and the weather-wise predicted a big snowstorm. Shortly after leaving Christiania the snow began to fall, softly at first, and then thicker and thicker. It went on relentlessly till the train stopped altogether, and there was nothing to be done but to wait at Krylbö, a small Swedish village, and hope for the best.

After twenty-six hours' waiting the Karungi train appeared, but the snow still continued, and we crawled along painfully, clearing the snow before us as we went. The next day the snow stopped and it froze hard, the thermometer falling to thirty degrees of frost, Celsius. We spent most of the day in trying to convert this into degrees Fahrenheit, but without conspicuous success. Centigrade we knew, and even Réaumur was not unheard of, but what was Celsius ?

What fairyland it was that night ! I stood out at the end of the swaying platform in the strange enveloping silence that deep snow always brings, watching the train slide past deep black forests of grim pines bending under the heavy weight of frosted sparkling snow, and now and then glades of silver birches dancing like beautiful ladies in the moonlight.

19

The People Who Run

Up in those pure, silent regions the noise and squalor and clamour of the world all seem so far away.

*　　*　　*　　*

Quite early the following morning we arrived at Haparanda, the last town in Sweden, and just a few miles south of the Arctic Circle. Here the railway ends and very stringent searchings of luggage at the Swedish frontier were carried out. There seemed at first no prospect of ever finishing at all, but at last the last article at the bottom of my kitbag had been taken out and thoroughly inspected and we were free. The next proceeding was to drive in a sleigh over the ice to the Island of Detention, a small island in the middle of the River Tornea, belonging to Russia. Here the passports were all taken away for examination and more official documents had to be filled in. Two hours to wait here, but no one seemed to be in any special hurry except ourselves, and so we, too, resigned ourselves to the inevitable and regaled ourselves with many glasses of sweet weak tea to pass the time. Then away over the snow again in another sleigh, the bells setting all the world a-ringing, and every bush and stunted tree a miracle of frosted beauty.

It was only half-past one in the afternoon when we reached Tornea Station, but a large molten sun was already sinking below the horizon in a blaze of glory, leaving a flaming blood-red sunset behind it. Ah! here was dear Russia at last; how good to be back again! Technically we were only in Finland, which is not Russia at all, as everybody knows. Once off the beaten track, Finnish and Swedish are the only languages spoken; Russian is hardly understood. But the railway-stations in Finland are Russian beyond all mistake. Here one sees all the soldiers in the familiar brown service uniform and hears the rich musical Russian tongue instead of the monotonous-sounding Swedish.

Here in Tornea was the familiar eikon of *Our Blessed Lady and the Child* hanging up in a corner of the railway-station, with a red lamp burning in front of it—a sign that we have reached a country where religion is a part of the ordinary workaday life, and where God and his Saints are familiar household figures and friends. How serenely they gaze over the excited crowd of passengers, the hurrying porters, the massed pile of luggage, the scramble for food at the buffet !

It must have looked very homelike to a stout young man who, very thankful apparently to find himself safe back in Russia, was crossing himself fervently with his lighted cigar, murmuring with great devotion prayers of gratitude for the safe return to his own country. One can only say of this incident that it was all very Russian and a more reverent proceeding than it sounds.

Two young English officers going to Petrograd, who were of our party, and who had been obliged, of course, to travel in mufti through Sweden, now changed into uniform, and the surprise of some of our fellow-travellers when they saw these two chrysalides emerging from the cloakroom as full-fledged butterflies was very amusing. Every one we had come across on the journey buzzed round them, and they had, as one Russian lady said, " un succès fou."

We sped swiftly for two days through the monotonous snow-covered pine-forest of Finland, passed the last custom-house at Beylie-Ostrov, and found ourselves at one of the uncanny hours of the night in Petrograd.

A Journey to Russia

Every hotel was so crowded that we were thankful to find a corner in the billiard-room of the "Angleterre." Next morning, early, we were wakened by the deep booming bell of St. Isaac's, insistently calling the faithful to church. The sound of the bells made me realize, even among my confused and travel-tired dreams, that I was indeed back again in the great grey city on the Neva. For the bells of Russia are the most beautiful in the world—deep, mellow, and irresistible, and I can imagine the Russian peasant in other countries being as home-sick for his bells as ever the Swiss is for his mountains.

III

STRANGERS AND PILGRIMS

IT is a strange, sad sight-seeing that we have
come to Russia for. Instead of cathedrals
and churches, we visit baraks, tenements,
doss-houses, lodgings, feeding-stations, fever
hospitals, homes, asylums—all the various
shelters where "the people who run" have
taken refuge. Instead of the familiar gabble
of tourists, you hear all round you the medley
of tongues of these other travellers, Lett,
Polish, or Lithuanian, whatever it may be,
and, many of them being unable to speak a
word of Russian, they seem like dumb home-
sick animals unable to express their wants.
Instead of the usual series of picture-galleries
and museums, you have instead the vividly
painted mental pictures of some of the saddest
people that ever were seen. One can never
get blunted by the oft-repeated tale of sorrow ;
almost one's heart aches more as one gets to

24

understand and know better the circumstances
and history of "the people who run." Not
that it is all unrelieved gloom : life is not all
tragedy any more than it is all comedy, for
it has pleased God, mercifully for us all, to
make the blue sky bigger than the biggest
cloud, so that even in the worst event we can
always mingle one smile along with our tears.
Here the golden thread of heroism which is
woven in and out of the pattern of these
people's lives often relieves the darkness of
the rest of the design. Again, it must be
remembered that their sorrow is no sordid
one ; it is grand, romantic, tragical, and it is
a vicarious one, for they have suffered and
died in order that our homes, our country, our
children shall be safe. Can we suppose that
the Poles, the Letts, the Esthonians, the
Lithuanians, and the others cared over-much
about the death of an Austrian Archduke?
They have suffered all this, not for any fault
of their own, or because of any quarrel, or
even any particular interest of their own, but
simply for the common good of all the Allied
nations.

Many are the stories of the wonderful trek,
and they all have a grim fascination about

them. No one can be blamed for the lack of organization. The Russian retreat will live in history as one of the finest and most heroic ever effected, but at what a terrible cost, both for soldiers and civilians !

Some of the refugees travelled for weeks towards the interior on cattle-trucks, feeding perhaps only three or four times in a week. And these were the lucky ones, for many were too far from the railways to be able to use them at all.

These truck-loads of human freight were mainly composed of women, children, and old folk, as some of the men were already away at the war, and many had been seized by the Germans and kept to dig trenches or make roads.

This journey into the interior often took weeks, for the refugee trains stopped sometimes several days at a station or wayside halt. The railways were congested by troops and munition-wagons, Red Cross trains with wounded, trains with prisoners, trains with reinforcements, trains with richer folk who could pay for their seats ;—all these of necessity took precedence over the refugee trains. Some of the scenes in the railway-trucks almost

defy human imagination. Lunatic asylums
in the line of advance had to be emptied of
their unfortunate occupants, isolation hospitals contributed their quota` of cholera,
typhus, and almost every other known disease
to the outside world. The trucks were, you
would have said, as full as they could hold
with these, and yet at every little station there
was a crowd of fugitives waiting to be taken
off, and they squeezed and pushed their way
in, with their bundles and their babies, and
found room somehow among the rest. At
Ligovo one of the refugee trains remained
three days, during which time three small
loaves of bread for every forty-eight persons
was all that could be obtained.

Drinking-water was a great difficulty and
cholera so prevalent that ordinary water was
too dangerous to drink. At all railway-
stations in Russia, *kipiatok*, or boiling water
(sometimes made in large cisterns with a wood
fire underneath), is kept going for the use of
passengers on the long-distance trains. These
make their own tea at frequent intervals, for
all travellers in Russia carry with them a teapot, tea, and sugar for this purpose, and at
any stop one can scurry across the platform

with the peasants, the soldiers, and the others and fill one's little teapot with boiling water. This arrangement was, of course, entirely inadequate for the masses of refugees who were crowding the stations, and very much suffering was the result, especially for the thirsty children.

The local authorities did all they could to cope with the need for food. For instance, at Briansk a system of giving bread-tickets to the refugees was introduced, but the bread had to be fetched from the town, which proved a great difficulty as no one knew whether the refugee trains would wait there an hour, a day, or a week. More than once it happened that some of the family went off to the town to get bread, and when they returned from their errand found that the train had gone off into the unknown with the rest of the family and the luggage.

Neither birth nor death can snatch a moment of privacy in times like these. Women about to be mothers went through their hour of travail in public, helped by their neighbours as far as possible; and even the dying had to be got through as best it might, unshriven perhaps, and without the last precious Rites,

28

but nevertheless consecrated to God and his
Saints by the bitterest suffering that the
human soul can be called upon to endure.

Some refugees remote from the railway
kept to the road, using for the most part little
country carts drawn by small, willing, over-
worked, shaggy horses. Sometimes for miles
along the road one could see nothing but these
long processions of country carts. Alas,
often before the end of the journey the horse
and cart had to be sold in order to buy food !

Many fugitives walked the whole way into
the interior of Russia, carrying the children
and a few belongings. These were in a very
bad condition when they finally arrived at
their destination, as the roads were often
practically impassable with the autumn rains
and mud, and food and shelter by the way
scanty and difficult to obtain. On one of
these roads a little family of four started out
bravely with the rest of the village upon the
approach of the Germans. The father and
mother both died on the way, leaving the two
children behind them. These kept up with
the neighbours as long as they could, running
alongside of the others, crying and begging
for food. The neighbours had little enough

29

to give their own children but always managed
to spare a little for these two poor little waifs.
They soon became too weak to follow with
the rest of the party and lagged behind. No
one noticed their absence, and they were
found by a later party of fugitives side by
side on the roadside, having died of starvation.

Many refugees were loth to flee far from
their homes, and hid in the woods near the
front for weeks and months, waiting and
hoping for an opportunity of getting back
unobserved to their own village. At last the
bitter snows of winter drove them perforce
from these retreats, and at Christmas-time
refugees from the woods near Dvinsk and
Minsk were arriving in Moscow in large
numbers. Who will hazard a guess as to how
they managed to exist at all and how many
of these unfortunates perished during this
time ? One need only look at them to gauge
the extent of their suffering : thin, haggard
scarecrows that a few months ago were young,
blooming girls ; sharp-faced, precocious children with hollow eyes ; and starved peasants
prematurely converted into old, old men.
Listen to the story of Marya Ivanova, which
will go near to break your heart with the

sorrow of it, and yet it is only one of so many —so many—equally poignant. Marya and her husband, Vassilie, had a comfortable little homestead on the borders of Russia and Poland. They had youth, health, a prosperous farm just beginning to pay, and four little children. Then the war broke out. Marya's husband had to go off and fight, but she managed the farm during his absence, brought a fifth child into the world, and kept everything going as usual for a year. But the time of anxiety told on her ; she aged very much during that time, the neighbours said, and there were many silver strands threaded into her thick dark plaits. Then came the *débâcle*. The Germans advanced rapidly, the village was evacuated, and Marya had to flee hurriedly one night with her little ones. There was no railway near the village, and so Marya joined a party of neighbours and took to the road, hoping eventually to reach the main railway for Petrograd, where her husband had relatives who could take them in.

It was a weary time for them all, but Ivan and Michael, the two eldest boys, of eight and seven respectively, were a great comfort to poor Marya, and she declared repeatedly that

31

she could never have been able to keep up
with the rest but for them. It was they who
carried the big loaves of black bread that was
their main support during these terrible weeks
and picked the wild berries and mushrooms
to flavour it. Marya always carried the baby
Olga herself, but Ivan and Michael used to
take the little Nastia and Mania by the hand
and help them along the road when they were
tired, telling them stories of all they meant
to do when they were men, and of how they
would all go back to the farm some time when
the Germans had been driven away, amusing
them and keeping them quiet for hours.

Then one day there was a river to cross.
There were many refugees on the road, and
they had all crossed the shaky old bridge quite
safely. Marya crossed with little Olga in her
arms and Nastia and Mania clinging to her
skirts on either side. Ivan and Michael were
following behind when a rotten plank gave
way and they both fell into the rushing stream
below and were drowned.

Marya felt that half her life had been
torn away, but she went bravely on,
though like a woman in a dream. She
never smiled now at Mania and Nastia,

32

nor slapped them when they quarrelled, nor seemed to take notice when the little feet flagged on the long dreary roads. She did not even scold them for drinking water from a stream one day as they passed, although they had always been forbidden to drink anything but weak tea or kvass with their black bread. But that same night, when they were both taken suddenly ill, she seemed to awake from her dream, and nursed them with a feverish energy and a passion of maternal love. In spite of all she could do, their little lives ebbed away rapidly, and in less than twelve hours she had lost them both from cholera. The neighbours were very kind, but Marya would accept neither help nor sympathy. No priest could be found, but she borrowed a spade and buried them side by side with her own hands. She searched in the wood and found two pine branches, and fashioned them into a cross. She laboriously wrote on a piece of paper : " + Nastia and Mania. Pray for their souls + " and attached it to the branches. Then she took to the road again in a kind of stupor, forgetting even to eat. She tramped along as bravely as ever, but now her breasts dried up and she had no

C   33

more milk to give the baby Olga. She had been walking for a fortnight and had got quite near the railway. Marya walked into the station, sat down on her bundle. And waited, and waited. At last a long goods train was seen approaching. Marya watched it till it neared the platform; then, without a word or warning movement, she suddenly flung the baby on to the rails, and was about to throw herself after it when her arm was seized by a soldier who was standing near, waiting for his train. She was held back, struggling, screaming, pleading that she might die too. Some other soldiers leapt off the high platform to try and save the little one, but it was too late.

What bitter news for her husband when he returned wounded from the front some weeks later : his home gone, his children all dead, his wife a hopeless melancholiac at the lunatic asylum for refugees in Moscow. As soon as his wounds were healed he came to the asylum to visit his wife, and one little meagre piece of comfort is his—the Sisters there tell him that his wife is much better on the days when he comes to visit her, though not even a glimmer of recognition is apparent. Vassilie bears his trouble nobly, heroically, and with the characteristically Russian faith in his religion that somehow all is for the best, but any one can see that his heart is broken.

"You see, Sestritza," he said one day, through his tears, to the Sister who was nursing his wife, "it is the little footsteps I always think about, the little footsteps that used to patter up and down stairs all day long at home. I never can forget the little footsteps."

*　　*　　*　　*

There are many other stories almost as sad that could be told at this asylum. That delicate-looking man with the sad, kind brown eyes is Pavel Pavlovitch, the artist. All his youth was passed in a farm near the River Vistula. He was always a dreamer, not quite as other children. He refused to be a farmer like his father; he must be a painter, he said. And his family were proud of his beautiful gift, though they could not always understand his pictures. Most of all he loved to paint the river—the mysterious, slow, tragic Vistula, that has so often been stained with the blood of her children. He knew and loved every phase of it—the pale silvery tints of misty

35

dawn, the sullen yellow-grey flood churned with white foam in the autumn storms, the deep ultramarine of the summer night.

To go to Paris and study art was his dream ; but they were so poor—so poor. He lived on black bread and cabbage soup and saved every kopeck. At last his opportunity came. A large art exhibition was arranged in a neighbouring town, and Pavel was asked to exhibit. If only he could sell his pictures well, he would go to Paris next year.

The war began a fortnight before the exhibition was open.

During the first invasion of Poland the Germans occupied the village for just ten days and then retreated, and when Pavel returned to his house after the German retirement he found that all his pictures had been burnt. His reason left him and he was taken to the Moscow Asylum, where he is tenderly nursed by Russian Sisters of Charity, who are devoted to him and immensely proud of his talent. And gradually, gradually, periods of lucidity are coming back, and the doctor hopes that one day he may completely recover. He shows visitors his sketch-book with pride. It is full of pencil sketches of the Sisters, the

36

doctor, the asylum patients, the orderlies—
and these are drawn with great skill and
spirit. The world may yet hear of Pavel
Pavlovitch, the Russian artist.

Another poor woman in a corner of this
hospital is an incurable case. She lies curled
up in a heap on her bed, her eyes almost
starting out of her head with terror, moaning
and raving incessantly. She will shudder and
cry if you go near her, and is only content
when the Sister in charge of her ward can sit
by her and hold her hand, and then for a
brief moment her tears cease, and the poor
tormented brain is at rest. She was a French
governess in the service of a rich Russian
family living at Warsaw, and when the first
bombardment began and the cannon-thunder
seemed to be coming nearer and nearer the
city, her reason gave way utterly under the
strain, and she had to be sent away to the
Moscow Asylum. She is daily growing weaker,
and one can only hope that her sufferings may
not last very much longer.

In some respects these human derelicts in
the asylum were the saddest cases of all, but
still many of these have long since ceased to
feel or think, and the burden really presses

37

more heavily on those who have to face life and make the best of it. Probably some of the people who feel it most are the very old folk, who must feel acutely the uprooting from the places in which they have lived all their lives and their forefathers before them. Some refugees of a very advanced age have been received. In Moscow an old patriarch of 109 arrived at the station one day, but the effort of moving was too much for him, and he died almost immediately after. There is, however, also at Moscow, a hale old veteran of 104, who is very cheerful and important, and quite enjoys his reputation of being the oldest refugee there. On the whole, the old women seem to have felt their misfortunes more than the old men ; at least, fewer of them seem to have survived them. The old men can be made content with a little tobacco and the company of their old cronies ; perhaps, too, they are a little more used to travelling and mixing with the outside world than the women, who seem to miss terribly their accustomed seat near the stove among their familiar household gods. Poor old souls ! one wonders how many of them will live to return to their own country. Probably few

38

only, as so many of the villages are destroyed
and the land burnt, trampled over and ruined,
that the peasants will hardly be able to support
themselves there by agriculture for a long
time to come. It is to be hoped that some
of the reconstruction work of erecting temporary wooden buildings in the devastated
villages, such as has been so splendidly carried
out in France by the Society of Friends, will
be available for poor broken Poland. The
enemy has turned a fair country into a dreary
desert in which no man can live. Of the
peaceful villages only blackened ruins remain.
Look inside one of the few houses that still
stand. " Pillows and quilts have been ripped
open and the down scattered about. Samovars
dented by heels of heavy boots are lying about
on the floor. Cupboards and drawers have
been rummaged with bayonets. What the
Prussians could not carry away, they have
spoilt. Whole forests have been hewed down
or burnt. Wide areas have been cleared for
fields of fire ; peasants' gardens stripped of
their produce ; potatoes, carrots, and other
vegetables dug up wholesale and carried
off." The churches have been destroyed
and desecrated, and even the graves of

39

their dead have been defaced with indecent ribaldries.

The deserted homesteads at the front are the saddest sight imaginable. I remember so vividly one Polish farm I saw there. The doorway was wrecked by a fragment of shell, but nothing else was hurt. The furniture inside was intact, and the family must have left the house hurriedly, for a baby's bonnet, a half-written copy-book, and a cup of sour milk were lying on the table in the kitchen, and just outside a cow was lowing dismally for some one to come and milk her. Perhaps soldiers had been taking cover in the orchard, for shells had fallen there, and there was not a tree left standing. The poor, unsightly, ragged stumps gaped out of the ground and the pretty pink withered blossom was all trodden into the muddy earth. There was a certain air of expectancy about the old farmhouse that aroused one's imagination, almost it seemed as if the spirits of the occupants were hovering round and trying to shield it from further harm. One longed to know who the family were and if any of them would return to the old place some day.

There are many stories told of the children

surviving while the mother has succumbed to starvation. "Somewhere" on the Polish front a regiment of soldiers was marching through a wood, and they found in their path a dead woman with a baby about two years old lying beside her. The baby was just alive and moaning softly ; so they picked the little thing up and fed her, and then buried the mother under the swaying pine-trees that rustle and moan out an eternal dirge for the dead. The regiment would not part from the baby, but kept her with them for months—until, indeed, they returned from the front. Imagine these big bearded fellows busying themselves with washing the baby, preparing her food, and taking her with them wherever they went ! Open-air bivouacs, night marches, bombardments, agreed with her, and the little thing thrived exceedingly. When the regiment returned from the front they collected among themselves a dowry for the child, and succeeded in getting together three hundred roubles. Two of the soldiers then wrote down the names of the officers and men on a sheet of paper and marched off with the baby and the money to the Petrograd Foundling Hospital. They deposited her there, making first the stipulation that at any time any of them who happened to be in Petrograd should be allowed to visit " their " baby.

The number of babies lost and abandoned in this retreat is an appalling one. There are now at the front Flying Automobile Columns whose chief work is to go round and pick up these poor babes in the wood. Countess Tolstoi was in charge of this department, and her column alone has picked up more than four hundred babies. They are collected and taken back to centres at the base till something can be arranged for them. In the Caucasus there have been more than five thousand children collected who do not know their own names nor that of their village. Most of these are Armenian children, and in many of these cases the women have been drowned, the men massacred by the Turks, and it is only by the kindness of some of the villagers that these babies have been rescued. In Petrograd a little *Preoot* (institution) for fifty babies is just being opened by the Tatiana Committee. These are all tiny bottle-fed infants who have been picked up at the front. There is much room for more organization here, and trained workers are badly

42

needed in this direction. It is felt very
strongly by many that Petrograd is the worst
possible place for bringing up babies, and
some of the ladies on the Tatiana Committee
have urged strongly that they should be
planted out in the country in small colonies,
on the system of the English Village Homes
for Children. It is their special desire that
these colonies should be kept as small and as
homelike as possible, instead of putting the
children into the enormous barracks and
foundling hospitals so much beloved at present
by many officials. This scheme is a very
interesting one and would be of enormous
value if it could be carried out, but there are
endless difficulties in the way to be overcome
first. Battles must be fought against red
tape, and more money, more organization, and
trained workers are all needed—particularly
the latter. Money can be raised somehow,
perhaps the great emergency will burst the
strings of red tape, but the lack of skilled
workers is apparent at every step one takes.
Russia needs, in the vast fields of work caused
by the war, more trained workers than she
can possibly produce herself. Up to the
outbreak of war Russian ladies of the upper

43

classes had not been accustomed to any kind
of work, but the war broke down all artificial
barriers, and now most of these are willing to
do anything they can. They have entirely
thrown off their old habits and work assidu-
ously for others, but the best will in the world
cannot entirely replace the training and
discipline necessary for carrying out any
enterprise of this kind.

IV

CHRISTMAS DAY AT GATCHINA

CHRISTMAS DAY found us on our way to Gatchina, armed with presents for some children living there in a large barak.

Christmas is such a beautiful festival in Russia. For weeks beforehand every one is preparing for it. Every square and market-place is full of little fir-trees, and the poorest peasant will contrive somehow to have a Christmas tree and a few toys and *pryaniki* at least for the children. Special dishes for the feast are prepared by the mother, and every one looks forward very much to these, as Advent is kept as a very strict fast in the Russian Church. On Christmas Eve, when dusk falls, they look in the sky for the Star of Bethlehem, and when the first star appears then the great festival begins. Carol-singers pass from door to door carrying home-made banners and singing carols about the birth

45

of the Holy Babe, and wishing every one a happy Christmas as they go. The beautiful hymn " Lord God, Save Thy People " echoes through the still cold air. Then comes the beautiful midnight service in the church, and afterwards the tree is lighted up, the presents are given, and the feasting begins. We had heard that the poor little waifs in this barak were not getting any Christmas festivities at all. This was not to be borne, so, with the aid of many kind friends, some hundreds of gaily coloured cotton bags had been made, and each of these contained a handkerchief, a toy, a spoon, and a few sweets, biscuits, or nuts.

It was a day when it was truly good to be alive, one of the rarely perfect days that Petrograd can produce in winter—on occasions. The sky was a pale northern blue, and the sun shone out bravely, endowing the whole city with light and colour and lighting up the deep azure domes and pale gold minarets of the churches. A fresh fall of snow had recently occurred, and a sharp morning frost had turned it all into fairyland for the occasion. An hour's run in a very hot, stuffy train brought us to Gatchina.

46

Christmas Day at Gatchina

The barak was quite near the station, so the pile of Christmas presents was carried there at once. This barak was just an enormous shed containing five hundred families. Five hundred families! Just think of it; a whole villageful of people compressed into one shed! It seemed, on the face of it, a physical impossibility, but yet there they were. The Imperial Palace at Gatchina is the residence of Maria Federovna, the Dowager Empress, and the use of this shed had formerly been to shelter the royal train from wet and cold the railway-lines were still to be seen running along under the entrance. The building was a good height, so a scaffolding had been built half-way up, forming a top story, making the whole place exactly like a rabbit-warren. It is difficult to say whether it is worse to live at the top or at the bottom. Underneath it is dark, stuffy, and damp ; above it is lighter, but the bad air rises from underneath and the fetid smell of overcrowding is very unpleasant. At the entrance to the barak a sort of ante-room is divided off and furnished with long deal tables and forms, and here the inhabitants of the barak can come to eat. Outside this, in the barak proper, each family

47

is allotted about eight square feet of space to
live in, and five hundred families have lived
already like this for three or four months.
A low wooden partition runs down the middle
of the barak, so that the people living in the
middle are back to back with their neighbours,
divided by the low partition. There are no
other divisions provided, but many of the
people living there have corded in their space,
and have covered the cords with quilts or
curtains pinned over it so as to make a little
privacy. Others, perhaps preferring a little
more air, had no curtains of any kind, and
therefore all the family life was open to the
public gaze. It appears that the sides of the
barak are considered a rather more aristocratic
quarter to live in than the middle. For
furniture the refugees have only what they
managed to bring with them, and as those
here are all from Poland, and Gatchina is on
the main-line railway between Warsaw and
Petrograd, some of them contrived to save
a good many of their belongings. There were
some families who possessed a bed, some even
a cupboard, two or three women had managed
to save their sewing-machines, here and there
there was a cradle for the baby. Those who

48

had no bed slept on rags on the floor, and a tin trunk containing the family's clothing was usually the only seat. The refugees here, being all from Poland, are Catholics, and it was very touching to see that, whatever else was left behind, they had almost always managed to save a crucifix or a picture of the Madonna, which was hung up in the place of honour.

Here and there was an untidy family, but it was pathetic to see the care in most cases which these poor people took to keep the space allotted to them tidy and clean. In the lower part of the barak especially there were some very dark corners, and the children who lived in them looked greenly pale and sickly, like potato-sprouts that have been kept too long in a cellar. And outside the barak was a world of light and freedom—a world where the sun was shining and the air cold and invigorating. In the park close by, other healthy youngsters were tumbling about in the snow, tobogganing, skating, sliding, shouting to each other, and laughing with the pride of life.

"Don't these children ever go out?" I asked one of the mothers.

" No, Barinia, it is too cold; we have no outdoor clothes and no boots and stockings for them. We left our village in the summer and have only our summer clothes here," she replied.

I looked round and it was true. The children were in their cotton dresses and suits, and many of them were barefoot, and I remembered then seeing two little boys just outside the barak, as we came in with the presents, who, having evaded the maternal eye for one brief moment, were running barefoot in the snow, quite oblivious of their little red toes, raw and bleeding from the cold.

" But they have been here three or four months now. Don't the children even go to school ? "

" No, Barinia, the schools can't take them, they are afraid. We have much measles and scarlet fever here in the barak. Sometimes three or four children die here in one day. I myself have lost two. But what is to be done ? Others suffer still more."

Words are little use when one is face to face with the bare facts of life, and it is no use speaking comfortable platitudes to these

50

people. The subject was dropped for the moment, for the cotton bags had now been unpacked in the ante-room and arranged in great, orderly heaps : pink bags for the babies, dark blue for the big girls, light blue for the little ones, gay handkerchiefs with the flags of all the allied nations printed on them instead of bags for the boys. The children were all crowding round to see—rather shy, perhaps, at the sight of English people, but their little white faces gleaming with joyful anticipation all the same. Such a crowd of them too ! I had horrible moments of anxiety lest there should not be enough presents, and wondered wildly what on earth we should do if there were not sufficient to go round, but hoped for the best.

We got one of the biggest boys, a lad of about sixteen, to arrange the children in single file all along one side of the table where the presents were set out, and to make a passage through the crowd so that they could return the other way. They were very docile and good, poor little souls, and quickly tumbled to what was expected of them. One by one they shyly advanced, were lifted on to the form, received their bag, and scuttered away exactly like shy, friendly little robins who overcome their timidity in a hard winter and venture near for food. Most of the children had charming manners, and, admonished by their mothers, they curtsied and said, "Spasebo, Barinia," and kissed our hands fervently as they received their present. One had a good chance of making a close inspection of each child as it came up, and it made one's heart ache to lift the featherweights of wasted frames with almost every bone visible through the scanty cotton garments, and to see the little thin white faces and hollow eyes speaking of insufficient nourishment and bad air. One also had the opportunity of observing the many minor disorders that these children were suffering from, that will probably become either acute or chronic if not attended to.

Here came two little tots hand in hand, unmistakably brother and sister, with sore eyes, the eyelashes so glued together with discharge that they could hardly see to take their present. Children with swollen glands, children with an evil-smelling discharge from the ears, a little girl with a bad whitlow that wanted opening, a boy with severe ringworm, nearly every child with sores somewhere, little

52

boys whose white faces and puffy eyelids spoke unmistakably of kidney trouble, children with devastating coughs that almost shook them to pieces.

What a tragic procession !

How I longed to waft some of them straight to England and install them in a certain cottage in Somerset that I wot of, feed them all on cream, and let them play out of doors all day long, till those wasted little bodies filled out, those white faces got rosy and sunburnt, and some light and joy returned to those hollow, hungry eyes.

The distribution went on, and the children's delight over their little gifts was indescribable. One small girl who found a bead-purse with two farthings in it inside the cotton bag was so overcome that she did not know whether to laugh or cry, but finally decided on a beaming smile, with one large tear rolling down her cheek, which she carefully wiped away with a scanty wisp of hair lest it should splash on to the precious purse.

It is horrible to see a really hungry child.

Some of the children ate the biscuits like little starving animals. Others, having forgotten almost how to eat, had no appetites,

53

and just nibbled at the biscuits and then stored them away carefully for future use. Alas that there were only four or five of these in each bag !

In the middle of the distribution there was a strange interruption. A little procession of eight or ten women, chanting a mournful litany, pushed through the crowd of children and went out at the farther door of the barak. They were walking in couples and the first two were carrying lighted candles, and I could see that one of the women's faces was blistered with tears. A child in the barak had just died, and these women were going out into the town to beg some money for a coffin. We stopped the distribution and stood silent for a moment as they passed through, but it cast no gloom on the proceedings ; these children are too much accustomed to death to have much fear of it.

Our fears were groundless : the bags held out well. There were enough for every child present to have one, and a few over for those in bed who were too ill to come down and receive them.

Nominally, the refugees in the barak are supposed to report any illness that occurs,
54

and if it is of a serious nature, again they are *supposed* to be taken off to the hospital, but as a matter of fact neither of these things happens. The thing these poor people dread more than anything else is to be parted from their friends, so they conceal illness as much as they possibly can. No germ could wish for a better soil to flourish in than this bárak, and so the moment infectious disease appears, in the twinkling of an eye it is wafted all round the place, and the local hospital would certainly be over-full if they received them all. The refugees' horror at the thought of being parted from each other can be well understood. They have gone through so much, and have lost practically everything they possess, excepting each other, that to have friends around them who have come even from the same village, perhaps, is a great alleviation of their woes. For this reason, frequently, where better quarters can be obtained for them, they refuse the offer without hesitation if it is a question of being separated, or means a breaking up of the family.

Ordinary Russian town hospitals are drab, cheerless places; and, alas, in too many, very little nursing and attention are given to the

55

patients unless the tips are fairly frequent, so that there is a great dread among the refugees of being carried off there.

There is also the dread of returning and finding the family gone off into the unknown, and this is no idle fear, it has happened only too often.

Small wonder that they conceal and deny illness as far as possible, but in consequence of this, on the day of our visit there were cases of scarlet fever, small-pox, measles, mumps, erysipelas, and ringworm, besides other non-infectious diseases.

On going round the barak we passed the place where the little dead baby was laid out. She lay on the bed, dressed in a new bright pink frock which was only too sadly needed for the living, and new white socks and shoes, covered with silver paper, covered her little feet. A wreath of pink artificial roses was placed round her head, and a little picture of Our Lady of Sorrows, looking pitifully down at the heart-broken mother, hung just over the bed. The baby's little waxen face looked peaceful and happy, the lips parted in a half-smile.

On the same side was another cubicle where

a mother was leaning over the cradle of her dying baby, sobbing bitterly. "That is her last child," a neighbour said sorrowfully; "she had four and now there are none left."

"Can't a doctor be got *somehow* to look after all these children?"

"We sent for the doctor, Barinia, but he was away and the *feldcher* came instead. He said the baby had measles and inflammation of the lungs and nothing could be done."

The *feldcher* is a hybrid sort of creature that does not exist in England. He is somewhat higher in rank than a medical student and somewhat lower than a doctor. He never gets any further but remains a feldcher all his life, and either becomes an unqualified assistant to a doctor or takes the whole medical practice in a village where there is no doctor. Sometimes he is an old soldier who has worked in the military hospitals and knows something of rough surgery, but he usually knows no more of children's ailments than a chimney-sweep knows of Chinese porcelain.

"The babies are all dying here, Barinia," the woman went on, wiping away the tears, which were rolling down her cheeks as she

57

spoke, with her coarse apron. "They get very weak and they die. And sometimes they get very hot, and then they die too. Ei, ei, ei, what is going to become of us all?" and the poor woman broke down altogether and sobbed.

"But doesn't the doctor ever come himself?"

"Yes, Barinia, he comes sometimes and gives medicine, but they die all the same. Ei, ei, ei. What will become of us all? Ei, ei, ei."

In one of the little cubby-holes on the scaffolding above, a tall, gaunt man lay dying of consumption. He sat up in bed, supported by as many improvised pillows as could be obtained, with livid cheeks, purple lips, and gasping for breath. Still he was fairly cheerful, and was delighted when we gave him one of the children's bags. He was very tickled at being considered a child, and solemnly laid out the spoon, sweets, and handkerchief on the side of the bed. It was evident that the end was not far away, yet in the meantime he was a source of acute infection to his own family and all those round him.

58

Christmas Day at Gatchina

It would be difficult to imagine any set of people with less resistance to disease than the people of this barak after three or four months' residence in this place. They almost never get out of the fetid atmosphere, these people who are accustomed to an open-air, country life in the much milder country of Poland ; they are underfed and insufficiently clothed. Small wonder that they are ready to take any disease that presents itself to them.

Something indeed must be done here, and that soon, before they all perish utterly.

The barak in which these people live has been provided by the railway. A vast amount of refugee work has been accomplished by the railway people, who have strained every nerve to cope with the terrible distress that has met them on every side. Bad and horrible as the conditions in this barak are, at least the refugees have been given a free roof over their heads, and at least their shelter is warm—indeed very warm. The railway authorities, in addition, provide a sum of fourteen roubles a month for each family ; so indeed it is true, as one of the women said, that other fugitives suffer more than they. There are, for instance, refugees still hiding in the woods near the

59

front, prowling by night round their burnt, deserted homes, living on what they can get.

It is a weak point in this present arrangement that people with small families are much better off than people with large ones, as each family receives the fourteen roubles a month, irrespective of the number of mouths there are to fill.

A little organization here would enable the refugees to be much better fed on their fourteen roubles a month. As regards buying power in the present time, this is equivalent to about 4s. 6d. a week in England—not a very extensive sum on which to bring up a family, although Russians and Poles of the poorer classes live much more simply than ours do in England.

One of us asked what time they had their meals in the barak.

" We only eat once a day," the woman answered quite uncomplainingly. " We eat at midday and have tea in the morning and again in the evening."

" Can you not get milk for the children ? "

" No, Barinia, milk is too scarce and too dear ; we cannot get milk."

Instead of each woman buying and cooking

60

Christmas Day at Gatchina

her own little bit for her family, if some system of co-operative housekeeping could be arranged here provisions could be bought at a wholesale price, and the same amount of money would provide a much greater variety and supply of meals. I am not at all sure that they would like such an arrangement as well as the present one ; the little bit of shopping and cookery makes them feel more at home and gives them a little interest in life, and the individuality of choice and method is much better for them morally than being taken in and done for by others. I have seen baraks in other places which are much better looked after, which are cleaner and less crowded, and where meals are provided by various organizations for the refugees ; and as there is very little left for the women to do, they naturally look much more apathetic and unhappy than the women in the Gatchina Barak, bad as it is.

But I am sure that the advantages of the co-operative housekeeping would outweigh any disadvantages, and some method might be devised by which the women managed this between themselves, and either took it in turns to do the catering and cooking, or shared in the responsibilities in some other way.

The People Who Run

If only some benefactor would appear to enable those children to be got out of the barak somehow! If some building could be invented that would be a cross between a crêche, an out-patients' department, a kindergarten, and a feeding-station, where the children could come in the morning and stay till the evening, and be fed, clothed, taught, amused, and their ailments looked after, it might be the saving of very many of those little lives.

Since writing this chapter, I have heard that this barak has been condemned and the refugees evacuated.

V

REFUGEES IN PETROGRAD .

THE number of refugees in Petrograd, of course, fluctuates somewhat, but on January 1, 1916, this city contained 84,074 fugitives.

. Petrograd is the bureaucratic centre of Russia, and certainly if committees—and their number is legion here—have anything to do with it, then indeed the lot of the refugees here should be a happy one. But a large proportion of refugees have a way of slipping through the meshes of any committee, either from ignorance or from pride at having to apply at all. The most important committee in Petrograd is the Town Committee or Municipal Committee for the Refugees, whose offices are in the Duma. This committee has large central depots where the new arrivals are received, registered, given their green refugee book, supplied with free lodgings for a week, disinfected if necessary, clothed, and fed.

63

During that week they are supposed to arrange their future, to get work, find permanent lodgings, or get relief from the Tatiana Committee or one of their own national committees. Perhaps if they are peasants accustomed to working on the land, they may wish to be sent into the interior of Russia, and in that case they are given a free pass to their destination. The lodgings were at first very difficult to arrange for the enormous number of refugees who were constantly going and coming, but some one had the brilliant idea of getting permission to use the Custom-house, which was standing idle, and the enormous hall, where all kinds of merchandise used to be stored, was very quickly converted into a shelter for the refugees. The dormitories and day-room are clean and well kept, and the food given to its inmates is particularly excellent. Some of the young students from the University have been giving up all their spare time to helping here, and the girl students have also done admirable work in keeping the young girls straight and out of temptation. Almost one of the worst results of this terrible exodus is the number of girls, little more than children, who have taken to the life of the

64

streets. The refugees at the Custom-house looked happier and more animated than in most of the other institutions I visited, and this must be due to the tone of the place and the excellent influence of the matron, for the arrangements are not particularly comfortable, though the place was clean and the food. which is all prepared by students from the School of Cookery, is very good. One of the large halls of the Custom-house was used as a day-room, and there about five or six hundred men, women, and children were congregated, the children happily playing, the others mostly listening to six boys who were playing the balalaika. There were many nationalities there : Russians, Poles, Letts, Lithuanians, and a few Jews. Jews arrive in Petrograd in comparatively small numbers, as they are not permitted to remain there more than a week, and they are very well looked after on their arrival by their own Jewish Committee.

Every nationality here has its own National committee : Polish, Lithuanian, Russian, whatever it may be, and every kind of help that is given them, whether money, clothing, or offers of work, is written into the green book which every refugee receives when he is

E   65

registered, so that it is practically impossible for any one to be receiving help from two committees.

Another most excellent piece of work done by the Municipal Committee is the opening of a School for Mothers, which is quite a new experiment for Russia and was designed as a means of trying to partly solve the problem of the terrible infant mortality. In other European countries the infant mortality is higher in the large industrial cities and lower in the more healthy country districts. In Russia it is the reverse ; the infant mortality is distinctly lower in the large towns and higher in the country, and this is because the women in the town have more education and know better how to bring up their children than the ignorant peasants, who still practise all kinds of superstitious horrors on their babies.

The School for Mothers is a resident home for forty refugee mothers, where they are carefully taught the best way of rearing infants. They stay there for three months —one month before the birth of their child and for two months after. Unfortunately the house is not large enough, and they have not

66

a sufficiently well-trained staff to allow of
the birth of the child in the home, so the
mothers are obliged to go to one of the town
maternity hospitals for their confinement.
When they return, they are carefully and
minutely taught how to bathe, feed, dress,
and weigh their child, and the great art of
cleanliness is laboriously instilled into them.
It is hoped by this means to diffuse a few basic
facts of infant welfare among these people,
who need the knowledge so badly. One of
the nurses at the hospital told me that the
babies in the home were weighed eleven times
a day. This really seemed like overdoing it,
but the doctor explained this zeal. Many of
the mothers have foster-children given to
them to feed as well as their own child. In
order that their own baby shall have plenty
they sometimes deny their milk to the strange
baby, with the result that it pines away while
the other waxes fat and lusty. In order to
prevent this the babies are weighed immediately before and immediately after each
meal, so that this trick is instantly discovered
if any one tries it on. The after-care of the
child is not forgotten. When the mother
leaves the hospital, the trousseau that she

has been making for herself and baby is given to her, and many last rules and directions for its upbringing. One of the sisters from the home keeps an eagle eye on the mother to see if she is carrying out what was taught her ; visits her regularly in her home—every week at first, and then, if the baby is doing well, every fortnight, till it is six months old. It is a great pity that this excellent institution can only touch such a very limited number of refugee women.

Besides the National Committee there are other special funds for helping the refugees, and the largest of these is the Tatiana Committee, which has branches of its organization in most of the large Russian towns. This committee derives its name from the Grand Duchess Tatiana, the second of the Emperor's daughters, who is patroness of the fund. This Committee possesses large funds, which it administers in various directions according to special local needs. Its special function is the general registration and housing of refugees and the maintenance of a large Inquiry Bureau for the bringing together of lost or separated refugees, but it also has many homes and institutions working under

68

its protection, some of which are very interesting to visit. There is a very simple but delightful home for fifty girls on the Vassilie Ostrov, arranged in what was once an old *traktir* (public-house). The house looks dingy and uninteresting on the outside, but one walks straight into a room full of happy chattering girls, aged twelve to twenty, and at once catches the infectious cheerfulness of the place. These girls have either no parents or have lost sight of them temporarily, and have been taken into the house and mercifully saved from a life on the streets. It is a very sad fact that many of the refugee girls have been ruined, not only by strange men with whom they pick up acquaintance in the street, but also largely in the huge baraks and lodgings, where the vicious and the virtuous alike rub shoulders. At this little home the girls have lessons in the morning, an instructor comes to teach them to sew in the afternoon, and the various ladies on the committee take it in turns to give them simple drill, music, or a little lecture in the evening. They learn to sew, machine, cut out, and make clothes, and not only do all the sewing for the Home, but also take orders, mostly from the Tatiana

Committee, for making clothes for the other refugees, and for this work they are, of course paid. Those who are earning money and can afford it pay four roubles a month (value 8s. 8d. before the war) towards their keep, the others are received free. The girls do all the work of the house in turn, and are placed out as opportunity occurs, either in domestic service or as assistants to dressmakers. It was a surprise to find a little girl of about fifteen speaking quite good English—and she also was delighted to have the chance of showing it off. She told us that she had lived in Sheffield for fourteen months before the war began, but directly after that the family had returned to Poland, her father being liable for military service. Now the father had been killed in the war ; her mother was killed also from a bomb thrown from a German aeroplane, leaving behind her a two-weeks-old baby and three other children, of whom this girl was the eldest. The little damsel seemed very happy here and delighted and proud to be earning a little money by her work.

The arrangements in this home are simple in the extreme. Downstairs is the large day-room, which opens straight into the street, and which formerly was the public room of the *traktir* ; behind it, the dining-room and kitchen ; upstairs, two large dormitories with spotlessly clean white beds (too near each other to be hygienic, according to English ideas) ; and that is all except the matron's minute bedroom, in which, in default of any other sitting-room, we sat for hours that afternoon, discussing, in fragmentary Russian, French, English, or German, the war and its consequences, with the matron and secretary of the home. It is a blessing that Russians are absolutely unselfconscious people. Some young men might feel embarrassed talking to two total strangers in somebody else's little back bedroom ; but not at all so was the keen and enthusiastic young secretary, who, happily for us, had a great admiration for everything and everybody English. He was, I am sure, entirely oblivious of his surroundings, and was one of those delightful people who are equally at home in a palace or in the kitchen.

He lamented that more provision was made for the refugee girls than for the boys.

" Do tell all your friends in England," he went on, " how badly we want homes for

refugee boys here, to be run on the English
Boy Scout principle. Here I don't know
how it will end. The boys are in the streets,
they are being taught nothing, and they are
only learning to be thieves. You in England
are specialists in the matter. Could you not
send us over some people who would arrange
such a home, and it would be a model for us
to copy. We Russians are very fond of
children, but we have no discipline ; children
need discipline and training." · Russians are
often very self-depreciatory, but this I believe
is quite true ; no Russian child dreams of
obeying his parents unless he happens to
want to.

" But we are also starting a home for boys
directly," remarked the matron.

" Yes, but it is only for fifty boys, and that
is almost nothing compared with the number
of boys running about in the streets, learning
only bad ways. It all wants organization,
and the English are such good organizers."

It was rather embarrassing to be expected
to know all the intricate details of the Boy
Scout movement, Barnardo's Homes, Father
Ban's Orphanages, and the industrial school
system, but I did my best to explain the

principles we tried to work on in England in
the training of boys, and anything I could
tell them was listened to with absorbing
interest. The secretary is a very keen educa-
tional reformer, and longs to have some really
big scheme in which he could expend his
really good organizing powers. In the new
school for refugees the boys are to be taught
ordinary lessons, as well as industrial trades,
such as shoemaking, carpentering, and so on,
but it is recognized to be at present an experi-
mental scheme only ; there is here again the
usual cry, " The money could be found
somehow, but there are not enough workers."

* * * *

The Tatiana Committee has specially interested itself in the very difficult question of
housing. Petrograd has fifty per cent. more
than its usual complement of inhabitants, and
many of the refugees have had to pay large
prices for a corner in a crowded tenement-
room. The Tatiana Committee has therefore
erected or utilized large baraks or wooden
sheds where the refugees can sleep. Miserable
enough some of these baraks are, and dirty
and overcrowded in some cases, but still they

73

have met a need, and certainly are less squalid than some of the common lodging-houses which the refugees inhabit. These seem to be the very epitome of vice, degradation, and misery; and the sight—and the smell—of some of the corners and glory-holes in these tenements are quite unforgettable.

A new and very interesting effort made by the Tatiana Committee is the erection of a little wooden barak near the Warsaw station to serve as a maternity hospital for the refugees. This is an institution which was very badly needed, as the ordinary maternity hospitals of the town are very much overcrowded, and in the baraks and tenements the women are too abjectly poor to be able to pay for proper medical assistance. Also, in these places, they live under such very unhygienic conditions that very few infants born there survive more than a few weeks.

The doctor, matron, and nursing staff for this new hospital have been sent out from England by the National Union of Women's Suffrage Societies, the Committee paying the entire expense of outfit, journey, and salaries, besides paying a large sum monthly towards the upkeep of the hospital. This Society has

74

had so much valuable experience in fitting out units for the Scottish Women's Hospitals in Serbia and France that their help is immensely valued here. The Grand Duchess Cyril and the British Ambassadress are patrons of the little hospital and take a great interest in it.

Schemes of this kind do more than anything else to cement our friendship with Russia and lead to a better understanding between the two nations. The Russian people cannot but believe in our disinterested friendship when they see us helping their refugees not only with money but with personal service.

The hospital is a plain little wooden structure, with fittings and appurtenances of the simplest possible character, but it must be a revelation of cleanliness, light, and purity to those women who come there out of the dark, noisome barak to give birth to their child.

It is a delightful work to be helping in, both for the donors of the money and for the staff. Russian babies are such particularly nice people. Our method of bringing them up differs very much from theirs. The Russian plan is to carefully preserve them from every

75

breath of fresh air, and swaddle them with
long bandages till they look exactly like the
old Italian bambini, but they seem to thrive
under this treatment all the same, when
properly looked after, and you can get the
most enchanting fat, contented smiles from
them if you approach them at the right
moment.

Another very valuable institution arranged
by the Tatiana Committee is the Home for
Lost Children, which is under the direct care
of the Grand Duchess Cyril. It is intended
to receive some of the poor little scraps of
humanity who were separated from their
parents during the first great eastward rush
and were unable to give any account of
themselves—and did not know even their
name or their village. There are many
touching stories told at this Home about the
joy of some of the mothers who have searched
for their children in vain through all the
institutions for refugees in Petrograd and have
at last found their little one happily established
at the Tatiana Home.

It is wonderful how some of these children
have survived at all. One little baby only
six months old was found by a Red Cross

sister at the front, lying on the ice-banks of the River Dvina. She must have been a remarkably tough infant, for she never seemed a penny the worse for her experience. The sister carried her back to their military hospital and they kept her there for some time, looking upon her as a sort of mascot that would bring luck to the hospital. Little Dvina ruled the men with a rod of iron, and every one was her devoted slave, but eventually the hospital had to be moved farther back, and they could not keep the little thing any longer, so she was transferred to the Tatiana Home.

In the early days, when the Home was first opened, the Committee suffered many vicissitudes on account of the epidemics of measles and other dire diseases, but now an observation home with forty beds has been started, where every child goes first for a fortnight, to be cleaned up and disinfected, so that these fell visitations have now almost ceased.

The Great Britain to Poland Fund has also a large branch here in Petrograd. This is a large relief society, supported mainly by funds collected in England, and is locally known as the Bariatinski Committee. The Society concerns itself chiefly with the feeding of the refugees, and under its auspices different feeding-stations, or *pitatelny punkte*, as they are called, have been organized. One of these feeding-points most interesting to English visitors is a large barak close to the Warsaw station, which is partly maintained and entirely staffed by members of the British community in Petrograd.

The building consists of a large wooden barak, with long deal tables and forms, where 700 or 800 people can sit down at one time. The average number of meals served here daily is about 1400, but as many as 1800 meals in the day have been served here occasionally. The refugees who come to this feeding-point receive soup and bread in the morning, *kasha* (a kind of porridge) and bread in the afternoon, and another meal of tea and bread in the evening, but this last is provided and distributed by a Russian society, the British community being only responsible for the two first meals.

At feeding-time the refugees begin to flock in, show their green book to the voluntary worker guarding the door, and receive a metal tally. They form up into single file and go up in turn to receive their bowl of soup or kasha and a great hunk of black bread, giving up their metal tally in exchange. The tallies are put in a bowl and counted afterwards, so that a careful record is kept of the number of people fed every day. The large number of people fed daily makes it possible to provide these meals at quite a low cost, in spite of the very high price of provisions in Petrograd. The cost has been worked out at about one penny per meal. The soup is excellent—thick soup with meat and vegetables in it—and is served very hot and appetizingly. Other Russian housekeepers have been heard to envy the refugees in this one respect—that they find these hot dinners waiting for them every day without any trouble on their part, when food is so dear and difficult to obtain. There is a certain amount of legitimate grumbling when able-bodied lads and strapping girls, quite able to work, come in for a free meal, but on the whole there is very little abuse of hospitality. There are always a certain number of people in every community who refuse to work, although they are quite physically able, and there are some of these among the refugees. There are also those

79

who argue, not unnaturally perhaps, that as
they have been obliged to sacrifice everything
for the general good of the nation, it is the
part of the Government to provide them with
everything needful and keep them in idleness.
This view is not encouraged by the most
decent of the refugees, however. An Employment Bureau has been opened for men and
women, and as labour is both scarce and dear,
they can very easily get work at good wages,
and so in time a good many of the refugees
should be absorbed into the general population. The mothers with large families will
have to continue to be supported by the
community, and these will be a problem long
after the war ends. It is these little future
citizens that it is all-important to try and
save. It is much to be hoped that the authorities in Petrograd will devise some means of
housing before long, other than the impossible
baraks and dirty, dark, overcrowded tenements that now exist. Moscow has partly
met this need by building a model village
about two miles out of Moscow, where five
thousand refugees can live. This, of course,
is only a drop in the ocean compared with
the wide sea of their needs, but it must relieve

the congestion in the city to some extent, and at any rate it is a step in the right direction. It has been found almost impossible to get the peasants to work in the towns. They have been accustomed to the land and to outdoor pursuits, and absolutely cannot accustom themselves to industrial or factory life. Many of the women sew beautifully and can earn a good deal of money by working for the Tatiana and other committees, as, of course, very large quantities of clothing are needed for the refugees. At the English feeding-point in Petrograd, a system of giving out clothes once a week to those who need them is undertaken, and has been brought to a high point of perfection. A very careful list is made of what clothing is most necessary for each family, and then the neat bundles are tied up and numbered, the number corresponding to that on the refugee's book. Every Saturday morning these bundles are distributed, and a record of garments given is made in the refugees' green books, which they are always supposed to carry with them, so that there is no overlapping or giving twice to the same person. To meet the great need of clothes at this barak, working parties have

been organized at the British Embassy and
elsewhere, where the ladies of the British
Colony meet and cut out, machine, sew, and
knit every possible garment for the refugees
at the English barak. This fills a very great
need, for the Great Flight took place in the
summer and autumn, so that very few of these
poor people brought anything but their
summer clothing with them, and many have
come from the much milder climate of Poland
and feel the cold very much. 1914–15 was
an unusually mild winter, but 1915–16 has
been one of the severest winters known for a
very long time, and in weather like this it
means, practically, death to go out at all,
unless one is really warmly clad.

The American colony in Petrograd is responsible for the maintenance of a Home for Lost
Children, which is doing very good work. It
is staffed by Salvation Army workers, of whom
there are a fair number in Petrograd, and who
are almost all Finns. Thus here every religion
meets on common ground in giving help to
these people who have so little and who need
so much. Much is being done, but far, far
more still waits for workers.

VI

REFUGEES IN MOSCOW

MOSCOW is naturally the great junction of the Pilgrim Way ; travelling from north to south or from west to east, the roads naturally cross here, and every race, nationality, and religion are represented. In England we are apt to think of them all *en masse* as either Russian refugees or Polish refugees, and it is amazing— at least it was to me—to find out how many distinct nationalities were involved in the Great Flight. Before studying the refugee question, I thought that Ruthenia, for instance, was a country in one of Mr. Anthony Hope's novels, and it may be that a few other people are equally ignorant.

Even among the Russians themselves there are many very distinct races, as different as Wales is from Ireland.

Among the purely Russian refugees Great Russians, Little Russians, and White Russians are to be found. The Great Russians are the typical Russian people. They inhabit the centre of the Russian Empire and are more numerous than any others. The greater number of them belong to the Orthodox Russian Church, but a certain number are Old Believers, or belong to other dissenting sects. There are comparatively few Great Russian fugitives.

The White Russians come from the Governments of Minsk, part of the Government of Vilna, Grodno, and Vitebsk. They are mostly peasants, and are the poorest and least advanced of all the Russian people. There are naturally a great many fugitives from these Governments.

The Little Russians are typical Southerners; quick, responsive, and imaginative. They inhabit Kiev, Poltava, Volhynia, Bessarabia, and are to be found in considerable numbers among the refugees. Their dialect, national dress, and customs are very distinctive.

Among the non-Russian fugitives are the people of the Baltic Provinces; the Esthonians, who inhabit Esthonia and North Livonia; and the Letts from Courland and South Livonia. Most of these are Lutherans,

84

and might almost be classed together, as they are very much alike in character, hardworking, frugal, and prudent.

The Lithuanians inhabit the plains of Lithuania, of which Vilna is the most important town. They are mostly Roman Catholics, and for this reason, when the first lists of refugees were made, they were counted in together with the Poles, but they are quite a distinct race and have the reputation of being very industrious and economical, which virtues the Poles are certainly innocent of. There are, of course, many thousands of Lithuanian refugees, as their country has been largely occupied by the enemy. Their language is Lithuanian, a Slav dialect. There are a great many Jews among the refugees from this province.

Probably more is known of the Polish refugees than of any of the other refugees in Russia, and they, of course, form a large proportion of the total number of fugitives. At the beginning of the war there was some anxiety among the authorities as to the attitude of the Poles, but the Proclamation issued on August 15, 1914, by the Grand Duke Nicholas, on behalf of the Tsar, was a removal

85

of their grievances and a solemn reconciliation between Russia and Poland. Their national aspirations were recognized and admitted, and the Polish people realized that the war for them would be a War of Liberation. The ukase gave Poland a pledge that her land, her liberty, and her national tongue, lost a century and a half ago, should be restored to her. This promise to restore what had so long been struggled for in vain, and the recognition of their keen sense of nationality, was to immediately arouse the truest sense of patriotism and enthusiasm for the war. Poland had to be sacrificed temporarily, but the suffering did not dim the fire of their loyalty. The history of Poland has ever been stained with the blood of her children, and the sense of tragedy lies over her yet. Russian Poland, being the " bastion " between German territory north and west and Austrian territory to the south, was the first country to be invaded by the enemy. Events followed each other so dramatically here that the eyes of the whole world were turned upon Poland in her distress, and the sympathy of all civilized nations is hers.

Among all these refugees there were

sprinkled a great many Germans : some, colonists and German subjects ; many, loyal Russian subjects but unable to speak any other language than German. The former have been sent into the interior, and as they are under police supervision they hardly come under the heading of refugees. The latter fled in large numbers at the German advance and have had a good deal to bear, having been constantly, and often unjustly, suspected of having German sympathies.

The Ruthenians—or Ukranians, as they are sometimes called—are Little Russians by race. They overflowed from Kiev and Volhynia into Bessarabia and Galicia, and form nearly fifty per cent. of the whole population of Galicia. Their language is almost the same as the Little Russian dialect, and they are naturally, although Austrian subjects, extremely Russian in sympathy.

When the Russians first advanced into Galicia the Ruthenian population there hailed their advent with joy, and when the Russians had to retire later on, almost the whole Ruthenian population fled too, for fear of reprisals. Their fear was not without foundation. In the second Report of the Great Britain to Poland

87

Fund it is related how, in a village near Sambov, twelve girls were hanged by the Austrians because they had sung a song of welcome to the Emperor Nicholas during his visit to Galicia. This report estimates the number of Galician refugees as not less than two hundred thousand.

Then there are Armenian refugees; not many adults, alas, as so many were massacred by the Turks, but a large number of children. A few Mohammedan refugees also arrive in Moscow from the Caucasus from time to time, but these are mostly sent to Kazan and the Tartar towns on the Volga.

Moscow claims to be the most progressive city in the Russian Empire, and certainly the way in which its various charities for the relief of the refugees are organized and co-ordinated goes far to prove its claim. The difficulties all through have been greater here than in Petrograd, as the influx of refugees here was much larger and more unexpected, and the daily number of new arrivals to cope with has been much greater. The Mayor and the Municipal Committee, faced with the terrible distress and urgent need that arose in August 1915, must have either mastered the situation

at once or have been entirely swamped by it ;
but they rose to the occasion, shouldered the
burden and the responsibility, and saved the
situation somehow.

At the time of the great flight the city
contained already far more than its usual
number of inhabitants, as troops, of course,
were quartered there in considerable numbers ;
and Moscow, with a university and large
medical school, is also an immense hospital
centre for the wounded. Food and lodgings
were already scarce and prices very high, and
the sudden influx of hundreds and thousands
of refugees, of course, forced them higher, so
that the ordinary poor of Moscow suffered
very much also.

These August days were terrible ones in
Moscow, as the refugees poured in like a
submerging tidal wave by road and by rail
and camped by the thousand in the railway-
station, and it was only by immediate organization that these people were saved from
literally dying of starvation. The Municipal
Committee commandeered at once every available empty building and put into action every
existing agency for the relief of suffering. For
instance, Countess Brodinsky's organization

89

had up to that time been engaged in working at feeding-points for wounded soldiers ; now, at once, they enlarged their activities and established large feeding-points for the refugees, and every railway-station soon had its own feeding-point, managed by one or other of the local committees.

The British community at Moscow at once co-operated with the Municipal Committee to help in the urgent work of relief. A Refugee Section was organized as part of the British War Relief Fund which had been started at the beginning of the war, and a large sum from the Great Britain to Poland Fund was allowed to the British Committee. Some members of the committee, accompanied by M. Gregorieff, of the Moscow Town Council, made a round of the railway-stations where train-loads of refugees were being brought in, dumped down, and left, and finally it was decided that the organization of the relief work at the Alexandrovsky station should be put into their hands.

The British Community, having gained this permission, let no grass grow under their feet. Within forty-eight hours the committee had obtained premises, furniture, an army field-

90

kitchen, horses, servants and drivers (almost all refugees), cooking utensils and provisions, and on August 22, two days after the committee had first met, the first batch of 450 refugees had been fed with soup and bread.

By the next day these miracle-workers had arranged for a supply of milk from the country for the children, and 1200 refugees were fed. By the end of the month 3000 refugees daily were being fed by the British Community, and though the numbers fed naturally fluctuates, this corporal work of mercy has gone on ever since. The total number of meals distributed up to November 5, 1915, was 140,450.

This large number of meals supplied proves what a real sacrifice this work has been in precious time, as well as in money, as every meal is supervised personally by one or other of the committee. The British Community in Moscow is not a large one, and the men are mostly engaged all day. Many of the business men have given up their lunch hour (and their lunch !) in order to help distribute the midday meal to the refugees. Their work for the poor fugitives they have taken under their wings goes on after business hours till late in the evening. To organize the work; the committee meets even after that.

For want of premises, the feeding at the Alexandrovsky station has to take place in the open air. Every day, about noon, outside the station yard, there is an expectant row of people waiting for the field-kitchen to rumble up with its savoury load. When I visited this feeding-point it was a bitter December day with the thermometer twenty-five degrees below zero and a searching north wind that penetrated any thickness of clothing; even my big sheepskin coat might have been made of tissue-paper. Life is hardly worth living on a day like this. The cold is like a wild beast waiting to seize you; you are unable to draw a deep breath, your eyelashes are frozen, and little prickly icicles are formed from the moisture in your nostrils and drip on to your chin, where they instantly freeze again. The refugees, their features pinched and reddened by the cold, and shivering in their scanty garments, stood huddled up together, patiently awaiting their dinner. How they could exist at all in this awful cold I could not imagine. Personally, I had a strong desire to depart into the warm

station building after the first five minutes
of it.

Hundreds of fat, conceited pigeons were
strutting up and down the square, preening
their pinky grey breasts and daintily picking
up the corn thrown to them by the passer-by.
They formed a great contrast to the crowd of
haggard and worn refugees, patiently waiting
in the cold. The pigeon in Russia is looked
upon as a sacred bird, since the Holy Ghost
came down from heaven in the form of a dove,
and the poorest refugee would not kill a
pigeon for food.

A faint cheer went up when the old horse
attached to the army field-kitchen was seen
trotting round the corner, clouds of steam
issuing from the big boiler, and the grateful
smell of hot soup soon began to perfume the
air. Two English ladies and a young Englishman were waiting there to serve out the meal,
and I think that this daily task, in which they
never falter or appear to be weary, is an heroic
one. They get chilled to the bone standing
there gloveless in the snow, noting down each
name in the list and serving out the portions
of bread and soup, but there was always a
smile and a kind word for each person as they

came up in turn. I have seen people doling
out soup as if they were in a ticket-office at
the railway-station, issuing tickets, or an
automatic penny-in-the-slot machine. It
must be rather more agreeable to the unfortunate recipient of charity to be made to feel
a welcome guest at the little feast. Some of
the refugees brought pitchers and basins and
carried their portions away. Others stood
round the tables spread out on the snow and
enjoyed their hot meal there, never heeding
the wind blowing straight over the icy plains
from the Arctic Ocean, which set a-fluttering
all their poor tattered garments. It was just
before Christmas (Russian Christmas is thir-
teen days later than ours), and therefore still
Advent. As many of these people keep
Advent as a strict fast, there were two kinds
of soup provided for dinner : thick soup, with
meat, cabbage, and bread, for those who were
not fasting ; mushroom soup for the others—
and each one as they came up said which they
would prefer. At the end of the long file of
waiting people was an old withered woman
who was fetching four portions of soup for
herself and her three little grandchildren.
She held out her pitcher.

94

Refugees in Moscow

" Fast soup, please, Gospodin, for me."

" There is no more left, grandmother. I must give ycu meat soup." She shook her head.

" You must take a little, at least for the children. Give me your pitcher, grandmother," urged the kindly young Englishman, who could not bear to see her go away empty-handed.

She shook her head again, too disappointed to speak, and tears welled up in the tired old eyes. She turned away sadly. There would be no dinner to-day, no hot meal for herself and the children who needed it so sorely, just because it was Advent and she was fasting, and the mushroom soup was all gone. Well, they would be physically cold and hungry, no doubt, but warm and satisfied spiritually. Truly these people make us ashamed ; they see so much better and more clearly than we do how very little the material things matter after all.

*　　*　　*　　*

The meal was finished, and the old horse trotted off with the perambulating kitchen, to take more soup round to various tenement-houses where refugees were lodged, where there was no kitchen on the premises nor any other means of feeding them.

Another feeding-point maintained by the British War Relief Fund, popularly known as the Log Hut, has just been opened in this part of the city. The building, which was opened early in the New Year, 1916, is the gift of the Spassky Copper Mines Committee, employés and workpeople. There is seating accommodation for 350, and it is proposed to serve a thousand meals daily.

The mere feeding of the refugees, so as to keep life in them, was the first and most urgent problem that met the Refugee Committee, but very soon the sheltering of them became a very serious question too. During the first weeks of the flight the weather was hot, and sleeping anywhere out of doors was an easy matter; but winter comes very, very early in Russia, and immediate arrangements for housing had to be made. As fast as possible refugees were being sent on into the interior; but, all the time, fresh ones were arriving in great numbers and had to be provided for somehow. All kinds of buildings were used; amongst others, some old doss-houses, in the Thieves' Quarter of Moscow, that had been

96

condemned and were about to be pulled down, were reopened and used for men. They were simply sheds with an upper and a lower story, and they contained nothing whatever except long lines of wooden shelves, with no sides or partitions, on which the men slept. A stove is used for heating the doss-house, and there is keen competition to get the middle bunks, which are the nearest to it. The windows were, of course, double and hermetically sealed, as always in Russia during the winter, and as nearly eight hundred men had slept there the night before, it may be imagined that the atmosphere was somewhat thick and stuffy. The floor and bunks were clean. Only small wooden pillows were provided, no mattress or bedclothes of any sort or description, so that it was easy to disinfect and keep the place clean. Just opposite these doss-houses were tenement-houses where families were lodging. These had once been old public-houses, and truth compels me to say that they were simply horrible ; dirty, smelly, and appallingly overcrowded ; two families in a tiny room with one window, and five families in another room with two windows. No one knows this better or deplores

it more than the Moscow Committee, but what
is to be done ? These people arrive and
arrive and must be put in somewhere. There
is very little hospitality offered to the refugees
by the residents, such as was so freely offered
to the Belgian refugees in England, where
people took whole families of them into their
houses. The reason is this. House-rent in
almost all the towns of Russia, and especially
in Petrograd and Moscow, is extremely high,
and therefore practically every one lives in a
flat, the people who inhabit a whole house
being almost as rare as people who live in a
palace in England. A family living in a flat
is in very close contact with the other members
of it, and not seldom they have no spare-room.
It is, therefore, almost impossible, except at
very great self-sacrifice, to take a stranger in.
It is very difficult for us to realize how in this
vast and enormous country it is possible to
hear it said so often, " There is no room." To
build is also very difficult. Wood is dear and
transport dearer, labour dearest of all ; but,
nevertheless, the wonderful Moscow Municipal
Committee has built a wooden barak village,
among the fields, a little way out of Moscow,
which will accommodate five thousand refu-

gees, and thus relieve, to a certain extent, the congestion in the city. It is built in separate pavilions, each surrounded by a piece of field, and each holding about four hundred persons, and the idea is not only to keep the family together, but to house those belonging to the same village together, as far as possible. The baraks are all built on the same plan : an entrance which opens into a very long dormitory holding about one hundred people and divided into cubicles by wooden partitions. Each family inhabits a separate cubicle, and this arrangement, though not at all ideal, gives at least more light, and air, and space, than in the old baraks, where there is generally a scaffolding half-way up, which forms a top story ; this feature has been omitted in the new baraks. The dormitory opens into a dining-room, and this again into another dormitory, so that the two ends of the barak share the dining-room in common. This room is simply furnished with wooden tables and forms, and acts as a dayroom only. The early breakfast and the evening tea are taken here ; the midday meal is provided for the refugees by one of the three large central kitchens, in each of which a thousand people can feed at

99

one time. Every effort has been made to
supply all needs here, although everything is
of the very plainest and simplest. About a
thousand refugees had been transferred here
at the date of our visit, which was in early
January 1916 (N.S.). One end of a barak
had been set aside as a home for about one
hundred old men, so that they should be
away from the noise and turmoil of the
children. These were already installed and
looked very happy and content. They com-
plained a little of being cold, but they were
accustomed to the much milder climate of
Poland, and the weather was certainly excep-
tionally severe, even for Moscow. The
youngest refugee here is eighty years of age—
a fine old type of Russian peasant.

Another barak was arranged as a bath-
house—one side for men, one for women—and
a laundry is arranged at the back of this.
Contrary to some people's preconceived ideas,
a weekly bath is almost part of the Russian
religion, and a function that the very poorest
never miss if they can help it.

There is also a school for the children, and
a large hospital barak which has several
divisions. One part is reserved as a little

100

maternity hospital. There is a large out-patient department, a ward for ordinary medical cases, and a cottage near serves as an isolation block. Thus the whole scheme is very complete and thought out with a view to securing the comfort and health of the refugees as far as possible. The health of the refugees has caused great anxiety in Moscow. It was feared they would bring cholera, typhus, small-pox, and other diseases with them, causing vast epidemics in the city. Fortunately, so far these worst visitations have been spared them, only sporadic cases occurring here and there, but there have been very severe epidemics of the less severe infectious diseases, and particularly of measles. The committees have tried to prevent the spread of this, and several houses, in different parts of the city, are being used as isolation hospitals. These, for the most part, are very dismal, melancholy places, although there are some bright exceptions. The mothers naturally dislike parting with their children, so these illnesses are hushed up in many cases, and the spread of infection still goes on apace, as any one may guess who has seen these crowded baraks and still more crowded, and much more unhealthy, tenement-houses.

The physical evil in the baraks is open and patent for all the world to see, but the moral evil that goes on in some of the dark, noisome tenements, with their filth-holes and dark cupboards, is veiled from sight and can only be hinted at and whispered. Those who made this war will have much to answer for, some day, for the souls of the innocent strangers and pilgrims who have been enticed into evil.

Moscow has made a magnificent effort. Every one is doing his utmost, but still more needs to be done. More money is wanted, more workers, more organization. One of the most delightful things about the Moscow charities is the harmonious way in which the different committees work together. English people so often have the reputation of only being able to work in their own English fashion, that the splendid way in which the British Community has worked with the local authorities has made a very solid and lasting bond of friendship between them. That surely is a great diplomatic triumph, though probably neither side realizes how great at present. There is actually a wonderful convalescent home here for 170 patients, in which the Jockey Club is responsible for the house and domestic arrangements, the British Committee do the feeding, the Ladies' Committee the clothing, and the Russian authorities do the nursing, and yet the whole goes on smoothly and without friction. Terrible domestic conundrums arise here now and then, which the committee have to solve. On one occasion the cook departed without notice ; on another memorable evening sixty children arrived unexpectedly, but every one rose to the occasion, and the staff succeeded somehow in feeding, bathing, and clothing the children without a moment's delay.

In Moscow, as in Petrograd and all the other large towns, numbers of infants and children arrive who are absolutely alone in the world, having been lost or purposely abandoned by their relations. To meet this very great need the British Committee have opened a little home for twenty orphans and abandoned children. It is all very simple and pretty. Toys and games have been provided, and the little ones seem really happy there. One hopes that they are young enough to soon forget the scenes of terror and misery

103

that they have been through. They will be kept here permanently until their parents are found, or they are adopted, or some other home is found for them.

A little report is issued in English, giving an account of the activities which the English colony have undertaken, and the closing words of this seem to sum up very well the attitude of mind in which these splendid countrymen of ours are working here :

" The Refugee Section feels justified in appealing to all British residents in Russia, and to sympathizers of other nationalities, for help in carrying out the important and urgent work it has taken in hand. It should be borne in mind that for military reasons these sufferers have been sacrificed for the general good of the allied nations, and all should unite to lighten their burden. . . . The work undertaken is considerable, but it is hoped by means of it to impress on the Russian people here in the heart of the Empire that their British allies appreciate the sacrifices made by Russia in the war, and that those who cannot meet the common foe in the field are endeavouring to do their utmost in works of charity and mercy."

104

VII

REFUGEES IN KIEV AND THE SOUTH

KIEV, as every guide-book will tell you, is the Jerusalem of Russia and the mother of the Russian Orthodox Church. It is also one of the most beautifully situated cities in Europe. We saw it at its very best, coming into it, as we did, in the sunset on a golden afternoon. There was deep snow everywhere, and yet there was the veriest hint of spring in the air. Everything was suffused with the golden flush of evening : the sky was the soft yellow of daffodil-petals, except in the east, where it was tinted with the clear, cool green of their stalks ; the river was the deeper glow of their centres, and the minarets all over the city looked like pinnacles of molten gold.

We were here, of course, to see the refugees, as Kiev considers, with good reason, that their refugee system is the best organized in Russia.

The People Who Run

The entire care of the refugees in Kiev is centred in the Tatiana Committee, who supervise every detail of its organization. All the special and National committees work under its central bureau—a great contrast to some towns, where each committee works at its own sweet will in water-tight compartments and no one knows what the others are doing.

Kiev is the Gate of the West. Being comparatively near the front, they had to stem the first torrent of the eastward-bound fugitives. By rail, by road, by water, they came pouring into the city. It all seemed so hopeless at first that it was difficult to know where to begin. Before one refugee train had been disposed of another overflowing train would arrive, and a special difficulty arose with the refugees who had fled from Galicia bringing cholera, typhus, and dysentery with them. It was a horrible idea to send them into the interior, distributing their diseases as they went, and yet Kiev was so overcrowded that it was manifestly impossible to keep all the refugees there. A portable army-disinfector was procured, and the trucks were disinfected after each batch of refugees had been received. It was a very necessary precaution, because in one day as many as forty dead bodies of people who had died of cholera on the way were removed from one of the refugee trains, and these poor refugees' ignorance of the language, their dirty and unhygienic habits, and their starved, apathetic condition made it very difficult for the authorities to impress them with the necessary precautions against infection. A dispensary was set up at the station, and all who seemed ill, or had been in contact with infection, were taken there and inspected by the doctors before being allowed to go on. The first great need was to feed the refugees, for many had not had a proper meal for weeks, and were, of course, liable to take any disease that was going. Flying feeding-points were organized by the Tatiana Committee in Kiev and the district, providing soup and bread and milk for the children, so that they should not die of actual starvation. Lodging was less imperative for the moment, as the days were warm and camping in the surrounding fields and woods was still possible.

Then the Kiev Committee did a splendid thing. Every one opened his heart and his purse and set to work to organize a thoroughly efficient hospital system for the refugees, and not only saved Kiev from an alarming epidemic, but also from the natural panic of the townspeople, who were very disturbed at the amount of contagious disease introduced among them. This organization was so well and thoroughly carried out that now Kiev boasts of being " the only city in Russia where special and adequate hospital accommodation for the refugees is provided." Empty houses were taken and fitted up as isolation hospitals, homes were opened for the lost children, disinfecting stations were arranged where baths and new clothes were given to all suspicious cases, and milk depots were provided where pure sterilized milk could be obtained for the children. These were locally known as " a little drop of milk " houses, and certainly saved the lives of hundreds of little ones.

One of the most delightful visits we paid in Kiev was to the charming hospital that has been arranged here for refugee children. Everything here is beautifully white and clean and pure. The walls, the cots, the furniture, the sisters' dresses, all are white ; even the stray visitor is not allowed to pass into this

White City without first donning a white overall. It was a great joy to see half a dozen convalescent boys tucking into their dinner with great zest, and such a fine dinner too !—minced cutlet, fried a delicate golden brown, creamy mashed potatoes, followed by beautiful pink translucent *kiesel*, a sweet dish made of potato-flour and cranberry-juice, which all Russian children love, and which is very easily digested. These half-starved children have to be very carefully fed, as they suffer very much from digestive trouble for a long time after. Down in the basement of this hospital " a little drop of milk " depot is being arranged, so that the children who go out and who still require special diet will be able to continue the treatment.

A certain object in a blue frock which matched its eyes, very small and very vain, adorns the wards. They do not know its name, so they call it Olga, and Mistress Olga is the oldest inhabitant of the hospital and the first child to have been brought in. She lay in her little cot for weeks apparently dying ; then one day she suddenly changed her mind and got better with amazing rapidity. She was playing with one of the sisters when we entered, but basely deserted her as soon as she caught sight of the big, black-bearded doctor who was taking me round. She staggered successfully across the ward without tumbling down, and then, clasping the doctor affectionately round the leg, imperiously bade him admire her new frock. Oh, the poor, poor mother who lost this fascinating person ! She may be still frantically searching for the little fairylike damsel, or more likely she is dead, as are so many of that army of mothers who left their homes in the west for the unknown country in front of them.

There is one big wooden barak near the station which has just been built for five or six hundred refugees. This is very complete, with baths, a hospital, a school, and a church attached, but in Kiev there are not very many of these big, crowded baraks and tenement-houses which are so common in the other large towns. The Kiev Committee believes in every one working who possibly can work, and being well paid for it too, and so most of the refugees make their own housing arrangements and pay for their own lodging. It was very refreshing to find so many refugees here busily employed. Even small boys of six and seven were being taught bookbinding in one of the children's homes ; a carpentry class for big boys was in full swing in the new wooden barak near the station. An old man was very busy making tin cups out of old Nestlé milk tins, and sold them at a halfpenny each. Refugees of the educated classes were teaching, looking after the children, and so on. But the biggest effort of the kind is the Tatiana Workrooms, where five or six hundred girls and women work. It has been arranged in the University gymnasium, and in the students' big hall a hundred and fifty Singer's sewing-machines are busily whirring. Nine women stand at a long table busily cutting out material, which is quickly seized by the sewing-machines and presently issues in the shape of shirts, dresses, chemises, petticoats, and all kinds of clothing. Even women with children are able to work here, because a charming little crèche for the babies has been arranged by the Tatiana Committee, as they do not believe in any one being idle. The cutters-out are paid 1.50 rouble (3s.) a day ; the other workers are paid by the piece, the average wage being five or five and a half roubles a week. The midday meal and tea

III

are provided here for the workers, and clothing is also supplied free to those who need it.

We just had time for a flying visit to the crèche. About six little babies were asleep in their cots ; about twenty more, aged eighteen months to about four years old, were sitting at a low table, drumming hard with their spoons and anxiously expecting their dinner. It arrived just as we did, and all these mites fed themselves with great dexterity ; even the youngest, who could only just wield her spoon, indignantly refused to be fed. Immediately after dinner the whole party went across to the corner where the eikon hangs, went down on their thin little knees, and piped out, in every kind of key, the Hymn to the Blessed Virgin, as a sort of Grace after Meals !

Another very important piece of work which the Tatiana Committee carry out is a Bureau of Inquiry for families who have lost each other. All the lost children are photographed, numbered, and their description written on a green card, kept on the card-index system. Parents' inquiries for their children are entered on a pink card in the same way, and so when the pink and green cards meet it means that the two members of the family have found each other. Up to February 1916 over fifteen thousand cases had been dealt with in this way. In the first week of November, for instance, there were fifty-three inquiries, and twenty-nine families were reunited; in the first week of December one hundred and eleven inquiries and fifty-eight families re-united, and so on.

The Great Britain to Poland Fund has an organization here, and we were delighted to find that the large sums of money sent from England were being so well spent. Like all the other committees, in Kiev this fund is affiliated to the Tatiana Committee and works in close touch with them. In the summer, when the first great rush of refugees took place, the Great Britain to Poland Fund took over the Contractovy Dom, or the big Sugar Exchange, which is only used for a month once a year, at the time of the great Spring Fair, and organized a feeding-point there for Polish and Galician refugees. They found a terrible state of chaos and overcrowding there. One of the early reports of the Society says : " During the first two days it was impossible to do more than buy and distribute bread,

H

sausages, and as much milk for the children as could be obtained, since the kitchen was in a state of dilapidation and it was necessary to build an additional boiler. The work was complicated at first by the fact that the building was overcrowded by a mass of Galicians, mostly Jews sent under arrest to Kiev on suspicion that they might give information to the enemy; but on the fifth day all those under arrest were removed, the Jews were cared for by a separate Jewish committee, so that the number in the building fell from over 2500 to under 1000." Even that is a goodly family to feed, but it enabled the committee to reorganize and improve the feeding arrangements. Three cooks were chosen from among the Galician peasants, and three other women assisted these. At the end of the first month over sixty thousand meals had been distributed. Three meals daily are provided: in the morning tea and biscuits, at midday thick soup made with meat and vegetables, and one pound of black bread (once a week meat is given instead of soup), and in the evening tea and *kasha* (porridge).

The report goes on to say: " The Contractovy Dom thus evolved from its original chaos, in which lurked the danger of a terrible epidemic breaking out, into an extremely useful clearing-house for the Galician refugees coming into Kiev, with sufficient sanitary precautions to prevent an epidemic resulting from the several cases of small-pox, measles, diphtheria, and cholera that occurred there. Of cholera there were only three cases during the first month. They were immediately removed to hospital, their clothes and other rags burnt, and their surroundings disinfected."

How to help the educated class of refugees has been a great difficulty all through. Most of these had a large or small store of money on which they kept themselves as long as possible. Some were reduced to very dire straits before they could bring themselves to appeal to any committee for help. One very wealthy Russian family was reduced to absolute beggary during the winter. Pride forbade them to apply to the Tatiana Committee, who would have undoubtedly helped them; they preferred to tramp from district to district, begging at private houses from time to time to get enough to keep them from absolutely dying of starvation. This, of course, was an extreme case, but there were enough of the educated refugees in Kiev to make it worth while for the Great Britain to Poland Fund to open a special dining-room for them. A school-house was provided for this purpose by M. Diakov, the Mayor of Kiev, who was immensely interested in the scheme, and the furniture was provided by the Tatiana Committee. The majority of the refugees fed here were University students from Lemberg, teachers (both men and women), and high-school boys and girls.

The third piece of work was the organization of a Home for the Galician refugee children. " This work was the hardest, but in some respects the pleasantest, accomplished by the fund in Kiev ; for the deputation had not only to furnish the house, have boilers built and clothes made in advance for the children, but they had personally to put up the beds, stuff the mattresses, and, by no means less arduous, to scrub the children, who did not take very kindly to what was for them probably an original experiment."

In the spring the Contractovy Dom was required for the Spring Fair, and the feeding-

116

point had to be moved. When we visited it in February it was comfortably installed in a large empty house, in a poor quarter of the town. About five or six hundred refugees were still being fed daily, and we were invited to taste their meal. After a long morning spent in seeing various institutions, we much enjoyed being refugees and eating the excellent meal set before us. We had happened to arrive on the weekly meat day, and fried minced cutlets, fried potatoes, and haricot beans were set before us. If the people in England who gave so generously to the Fund could be set down in Kiev at midday they would be rewarded by seeing the healthy appearance of the poor people here who are their guests. Would that their hospitality could be extended to some of the other towns, where the organization is almost *nil* and the condition of the refugees is miserable and pitiable in the extreme.

VIII

REFUGEES IN THE INTERIOR : KAZAN

WE came into Kazan in the late dawn of a
January morning. The wind blowing over
the frozen Volga was very keen and the air
clear and intensely cold. Everybody at the
station, getting out of the hot, overcrowded
train, was shivering and hurrying along to
try and keep warm ; the peasants, in their
orange-dyed sheepskins and brightly coloured
felt leggings, were burrowing into the hay on
their *barrabus,* or flat sledges ; ladies, in furs
up to their eyes and elegant grey-furred boots,
were shivering in their sleighs ; the Tartar
drivers, in tall astrakhan caps, were slapping
their chests to restore the circulation to hands
numbed with holding the reins. Only a
Mullah, lightly clothed in a green gown, and
with the white turban that showed he had
made a pilgrimage to Mecca, was strolling
along with a detached air, as if he were far

above such mundane trifles as a few degrees of frost.

At first sight Kazan is a crowded, huddled mass of roofs and towers, as Mother Volga makes a great curve here and holds the city fast in her maternal embrace, making a sort of moat or natural fortification.

Above us, white, detached, and remote, was the beautiful Kremlin, a formidable fortress indeed before the days of the howitzer. All round us were the blue domes and gold minarets of the churches and mosques. Early as it was, there was plenty of stir and movement going on. Housewives were busy chaffering with the pedlars in the Tartar bazaar; colliding mujiks in sledges were swearing lustily; the tinkle of the sleigh-bells, the shrill clamour of the trams, were mingling with the notes of the deep bell of Our Lady of Kazan; some Moslem on the tower of a minaret was chanting that Allah was great and Mohammed was his prophet. Kazan is one of the old Tartar towns on the Volga, and even now there are almost as many minarets bearing the sign of the Crescent as there are with the sacred sign of the Cross, and this same unfamiliar emblem is embla-

119

zoned on the flag of many of the hospitals for the wounded, too, instead of the Red Cross.

We were in Kazan because that is one of the towns in the far interior of Russia which has received a very large number of refugees. The chief business of every one connected with these "people who run" seems to be to get them sent away somewhere else, and whenever one asks, in Petrograd or Moscow, or in any of the large towns, where these masses of people are being sent, the answer invariably is, "They are going into the interior," so that no one who has not seen the refugees in the interior has really seen them at all.

Since the beginning of the great flight the province and town of Kazan have received almost more than their fair share of refugees, and even at the present moment there are over fifty-two thousand in all—more than four thousand in the town and forty-eight thousand in the province.

Like almost all the other Russian towns, Kazan was very overcrowded even before the flight began. It was a military centre, a good many Austrian prisoners had been sent there, and as there was a university and school of medicine, it was naturally a large centre also

120

for the wounded. During the first great rush eastward Kazan was almost overwhelmed with refugees, and gives one the impression of never having got over the shock. This overcrowding has produced the natural result that some of the refugees are housed fairly well, some badly, and some unspeakably badly.

Some of the dwellings for the refugees are entirely unfit for any human habitation. I shall never forget some of the people we visited the first evening we were in Kazan. Our guide was a young university student belonging to the Students' Sanitary Association, and twice a month he went round to all the refugee families he was responsible for to distribute the payments allowed by the town for their relief.

Our first visit was to a large family—or rather three families who were all related—of Old Believers, who were housed in the cellars underneath the Old Believers' Church. We found the church quite easily, but in the darkness even the student had great difficulty in finding the top of the staircase leading down to their dwelling. At last an old man appeared with a little flickering kerosine lamp to show us the way. The smell of sweating humanity, decayed food, foul linen,

121

and other filth that met us half-way down might have turned us back had we not by this time acquired a strong stomach. The cellar, when we arrived, was seen to be long and low and dark. There was a cooking-stove in the passage but none in the room where these three families were living together, and they required none, for the room was over-poweringly hot with the human exhalations, and the walls were moist and slimy with their breath. A few wooden plank beds, some wooden stools, and a few cooking utensils were the only furniture. The manners of the inhabitants were perfect. They greeted us warmly and begged us to sit down, as if they were still back in their own hospitable house. The student was evidently an old friend, for every one's face lighted up when they saw him, and his manner with them was charm-ingly paternal. He doled out a few roubles to the three women at the head of the respec-tive families, listened gravely to their troubles, and gave them good advice.

In the meantime seven or eight children who lived here shyly crowded round us, and as we had had the providential foresight to bring a few sweets with us, a good basis of friendship was quickly found. It is the sight of the children in these dens that breaks one's heart. What chances have the poor little souls of ever growing up decently in these surroundings? The older ones have at least had their day, but these are just standing at the threshold of life, and the scales are weighted heavily against them.

As soon as the student had finished we got up to go. They shook hands all round and thanked us warmly for our visit. The pathetic irony of it! To be thanked for spending five minutes in that fetid cellar in which these people, once well off and prosperous, had to live all the time—and we were well clad and housed and had three meals every day of our lives. The picture might have been reversed after all; it might have very easily been decreed that the horror of invasion should have fallen upon us too, and that we should have shared their fate. And all for what? For what? To gratify the ambition of a group of German potentates thirsting for blood and power. Perhaps if they could see some of their handiwork! . . .

*   *   *   *

We begged the student to allow us to

accompany him on his other visits, to see the worst baraks, not to be politely shown over the best ones ; and he took us at our word. Baraks, tenements, common lodging-houses—we saw them all.

In one of these a woman was in floods of tears. Her bread allowance for the day had somehow been put down in the snow and was sodden through and spoilt. It is easy for us who are well fed to smile philosophically over a ruined meal ; it is quite another matter when you are chronically hungry and the food represents practically all you and the children will get all day.

Outside the next barak was a group of Austrian prisoners clearing snow from the road. Fine, well-set-up men they were, very warmly clad with thick overcoats, felt *valenkies* on their legs, and knitted helmets, or cloth caps with ear-flaps, on their heads. Certainly they were in excellent condition, ruddy and plump-looking, very much better and healthier than any of the refugees.

The next barak was an enormous place where three hundred people lived together in misery—a terrifying vision of some horrible Inferno. Picture an enormous barnlike place,

124

the air thick and stale and foul. There was no furniture in it at all, except the wooden shelves, used as beds, that run all round the room, and some wooden boards on trestles in the middle, which serve the same purpose. The other beds are those heaps of rags on the floor. The filthy wallpaper was peeling off in great flakes, showing the damp walls green with slime underneath. Two or three kerosine lamps feebly illuminated the scene, which will be deeply graved for ever on the minds of all who saw it. A few half-naked children were running about, but most of them had gone to bed. We suddenly realized that these dark heaps on the floor in the dimly lighted room were people—men, women, girls, lads, lay about everywhere in uneasy sleep.

A little dead child lay on one of the shelves. Its mother, worn out with days of watching, lay asleep, with flushed, tear-stained face, by its side.

Suddenly the student, going first, stumbled over what appeared to be a bundle of rags on the floor. He stooped and found a very old woman, faintly moaning.

" Now, Babushka, what is wrong with you ? " asked the student, bending over her.

125

" I am ill, ill."

" Where are you ill ? What is the matter ? "

" I am ill, ill," she repeated shudderingly.

Such a sweet old face was turned upon us imploringly, the ghost of a plump, apple-cheeked old country-woman. Little could be done for her. The pulse was almost imperceptible, and a cold sweat broke out on her brow in spite of the heat of the room. Evidently she was fast nearing the end of her passage through this unkind world, and there was not much for her to regret in leaving it. She was alone in the barak, with no one she knew to watch her dying moments nor to mourn for her departure. She had escaped from her village at the advance of the Germans, with her daughter and her two little grandsons. Her daughter had died in the railway-wagon in giving birth to her third child, and the infant had been born dead. The old woman struggled along to Kazan with her two little grandchildren, but they both died of dysentery before they had been there a week, leaving her alone in the world. The doctor was sent for, and Babushka was tenderly lifted and taken to the room in the barak

called the " convalescent home." The name
was not given in irony. It really was the room
provided where those returning from the
hospitals were placed at first, until they
regained some strength. The convalescent
home was self-contained. It consisted of one
small room, rather cleaner than the rest of
the place. The furnishing was simple ; some
plank beds were all.

Just when we were going away, a woman,
seeing we were strangers, came up and caught
at my arm.

" Pardon me, Barinia," she said, " but for
God's sake tell me if you have seen my two
daughters. I have lost them and cannot find
them anywhere." Another of these very sad
stories of children lost on the way. These
were two big girls of twelve and fourteen years
old, who got out of the refugee train on the
way for some reason and have never been
heard of since. The poor mother did not
even know the name of the station, but she
had been waiting in Kazan more than three
months, hoping they would still turn up. We
tried to comfort her a little by telling her of
all the homes we had seen for lost children, and
about the Tatiana Inquiry Bureaux where

such gallant efforts were made to reunite families, but privately we could not help fearing that children as old as these were less likely to be found even than the little lost babies. Children of twelve and fourteen who get out of a train for food or perhaps because others did, who knew their name and where they were bound for, would certainly be sent on to their destination by the next train unless they fell into bad hands, which we could not help fearing must have happened in this case.

From barak to tenement we went, and there seemed to be no end to the flotsam and jetsam of human misery and degradation. We said something of this kind to the student.

" Oh, but you have not seen the worst baraks," quoth he.

" Then where, in Heaven's name, are the worst baraks if we have not seen them ? " we asked.

" We got them condemned by the authorities and have taken the people off down to our colony."

" What is your colony ? "

And then we heard the whole story of a most wonderful movement in connexion with the refugees. When the first rush of refugees came to Kazan volunteers were asked for, to help in the feeding and distributing of them, and in making the weekly or fortnightly payments. Amongst others, some of the students offered to help, thinking it would be only a temporary affair. They were put on duty at the various stations, and the sight of these helpless truck-loads of humanity arriving, stirred them to the heart. The work gripped them ; they were taken outside themselves altogether. They formed themselves into a Students' Sanitary Association : not a romantic name, but a very gallant and knightly venture. One of the professors at the University was the president, and they were all giving up every moment of their leisure to this work. The municipal authorities wisely appointed them as their official agents to help carry out the relief work, and part of their duties were to distribute the Government grant to the Russian section of the refugees.

Owing to the horrible state of overcrowding in Kazan itself, the students formed a colony of refugees away out on the banks of the Volga, in huts and baraks that were used as shops and lodgings for the summer visitors when the fair took place. And there ten of them were living, taking it in turns to be there, dressed in sheepskins and valenkies like the peasants, living actually with the refugees and sharing their food.

They were very anxious that we should go and see this colony, and naturally we were only too glad to get the chance. Horses were ordered for the next day, and in the afternoon we started off. We were wearing thick leather coats lined with sheepskins, but the students only laughed at these and said we should be cold, and went off to borrow *shubas* to put on top of them. Mine was an immensely heavy cloth shuba, lined with wolfskin, and with an enormous hood to put over my head. We could none of us move when we were shrouded in these things and had to be almost lifted into the sleighs, but we were very glad of them, all the same, afterwards, for there were eighteen degrees of frost centigrade and it certainly *was* very cold. We soon got outside the town and were driving over what seemed to be limitless snow-plains. The short winter afternoon faded, and we were driving by snowlight—and just two very bright stars,

130

low down in the sky, which seemed unfamiliar to us. The professor explained that it was Jupiter married to Venus, which only occurred once in hundreds of years, and that last time it happened Ivan the Terrible had died. What will it bring this year?

In this part of the country the howling of the wolves far off may sometimes be heard at night. We listened for them, but heard nothing but the thudding of the horses' hoofs as they galloped over the snow. Presently we seemed to be going down the side of a cliff. The sleigh swayed from side to side and the one behind us turned right over, depositing its occupants in the snow. Then we came to flat ground again. We were driving over the frozen Volga and could just see the dark outline of the low banks on the other side marking the breadth of this mighty river.

The horses were very fresh and excited by the cold and flew along. At last we saw some little twinkling lights.

" There is our colony," cried the students, and presently we had come to it, and a tall student, dressed like a peasant, with a horn lantern in his hand, was unpacking us from the sleighs.

The People Who Run

There were little houses dotted about everywhere on the river-bank. These were shops in the summer for the visitors who came down there, and lodgings, too, for the drivers, pedlars, and traders who came for the summer fair. These were now all used as lodgings for the refugees.

" All the refugees here are Russians, mostly from the Minsk Government," said our guide.

There was only one large barak, and that we visited first. It was then rather late and they were almost all in bed, but apparently quite pleased to see visitors all the same.

It was a great barnlike place, like the one we visited the night before, but what a contrast ! The air was fresh instead of being steamy and foul, the floors were clean, the walls newly whitewashed. There were only plank beds certainly, but the families were divided off by low wooden partitions, and they all had blankets and clean, strong, warm clothing. A small boy, who ought to have been in bed, was running about with nothing but his shirt on, and he had bright eyes and a good colour, and was as plump as a chicken.

There was one very beautiful thing about this barak. There was no church anywhere near for the refugees to attend, so the resourceful students used this barak as a church on Sundays and got a priest over. They had made one end of the barak as the Holy Place, nailed up blue linen to cover the rough whitewash, and hung up a great crucifix upon this. Underneath were little pictures of Our Blessed Lady, Seraphim, the hermit-saint, and St. George with his dragon breathing huge tongues of flame. Little red lamps were burning in front of them, and a wreath of artificial roses lay at the foot of the crucifix. All very simple and poor.

Instead of screening this off during the week, as nine people out of ten would have done, on the contrary the students carefully arranged the beds so that every one of the sixty or seventy people there could lie in bed at night and watch the great crucifix, dimly illuminated by the little red, twinkling lamp, and Mary keeping guard over the sleepers.

"If these are the same people we saw in town, why are they so much better off here? How is it they can have good clothes, and why is everything so much more comfortable?" was our first most natural question.

133

" Mostly because they all work here. We see that they all have something to do, according to their capacity, and then they are paid for it and can buy little comforts for themselves. We work ourselves, with them, and that encourages them. Come and see our bakery."

We went down some steps, sniffing the luxurious smell of new bread, and found ourselves in an enormous bakery. Shelves of loaves on either side—large black loaves on one side that a child could hardly have lifted, smaller white loaves on the other side ; and a lad at the kneading-trough, very hot and panting, being initiated into the mysteries of bread-making by the master-baker, who was an Austrian prisoner. We spoke a few words to him in his own language, and he told us he was very happy here and every one very kind to him.

" We make all the bread here for the prisoners and also for the refugees. It is excellent bread," said the tall student, cutting off a piece for us to try. And it was certainly splendid bread ; the old Austrian prisoner was a great craftsman. Then we were taken off to see the butchery department—a depart-

134

ment of domestic life always very repulsive to me, but we were expected to admire it; also the tailoring, where the clothes are made; the bootmaking, where great bunches of undyed skins were hanging from the ceiling; the carpentering-shed, and all the other splendid activities that are being carried on. It was perfectly delightful to see how the students were loved and trusted. To give money to the refugees is one thing; to actually live with them and share their life is quite another.

We ended up with the little room which was given up to the students—their office, telephone-room, dining-room, and dormitory all in one. There were ten beds in a row, with one single grey blanket on each, and no pillow.

" Oh, we sleep so well here that we don't need a pillow; we put our heads on our fists," was the answer to that.

It was about ten o'clock by that time, and we sat down with them to supper. There were not enough chairs, so we sat on the students' beds and shared their simple supper of butterless bread and milkless tea. I have never enjoyed a meal more. Their infectious, bubbling-over cheerfulness made us all very frivolous, and one of the professors who had come with us insisted upon trying to speak English, and made every one roar with laughter every time he opened his mouth. The students rarely have visitors in their colony, so they made the most of us and kept pressing us to stay, and we were equally anxious to hear every detail of their work. It was all hours of the night before we finally tore ourselves away from this truly inspiring place and got packed up in our sleighs again.

There is one very sad side to this colony on the Volga. In the spring the river melts, the floods come, and none of those houses and shops are habitable ; in the summer they are wanted for other purposes, and from May to October the University is closed, and there will be no students to look after the colony. The students have also arranged a little hospital for children with measles, which is the very apple of their eye and joy of their heart, and that, too, will have to be closed during the long vacation. So very soon these "people who run" will once more have to be true to their name and move on somewhere else.

Where ?

Refugees in the Interior: Kazan

Who knows ?

Anywhere.

But at least we may perhaps hope that these few happier months will have given them strength and courage to begin again somewhere else.

The students only look after the purely Russian refugees. Each National committee looks after its own people, more or less well, according to its lights and its means. There is a curious assortment of refugees in Kazan, Russians, Letts, Lithuanians, Jews, Poles, Armenians, and Mohammedans. These latter come from the Caucasus and are looked after by a Tartar committee. We visited one or two of them. In one house there was a poor little hen-pecked husband with four large, handsome wives. They had been very rich once and now were reduced to beggary.

The Polish Committee seemed the best organized here. Their baraks were well arranged and clean, and were visited by a doctor several times a week. There was a dining-room in the basement and a school for the children.

There is an Infants' Welfare Society in Kazan that ought to be doing good work ; it certainly has a grand field for its labours. It has very beautiful ideals but very, very scanty funds. An invalid-diet kitchen for sick refugee children who cannot take the ordinary food is one of its unfulfilled dreams.

This society is also responsible for inspecting, from time to time, some of the childrens' homes and orphanages in the neighbourhood. We visited one of these, out in the country, for girls and infants. The vice-president of the society is very keen to get the children away from the overcrowded towns into the country. A few versts beyond this home is a large monastery where fifty or sixty orphan boys from twelve to sixteen are taken and looked after by the monks of the monastery and a Sister of Charity who acts as a sort of matron. It was delightful to see the clean, airy dormitory and the great spacious living-rooms of the old monastery. One of the accomplishments of the boys is the exquisite church singing which they are taught by one of the monks. They sang the Russian Hymn to the Blessed Virgin and the Russian National Anthem for us, and as the clear boyish trebles of these healthy, high-spirited lads rang out, one rejoiced to think that they at least had some future to look forward to and had escaped the fate of many others of the fugitives.

* * * *

Another town in the interior which has received a great many refugees is Nijni Novgorod. Here East meets West at the great fair which takes place in June, where Tartar pedlars, Persian carpet merchants, Siberian fur-traders, Jewish hawkers of all kinds, Greek jewellers, Chinese tea merchants, Russians, Teutons, Scandinavians with articles of Western civilization, all meet. Great buildings line the left side of the Volga where the great Fair takes place. These Fair buildings are empty all the rest of the year, and so it was in the natural order of things that they should be used for housing the refugees. Alas, though, like Kazan, the Volga overflows its banks in the spring, and the Fair buildings are all flooded and unfit for human habitation till the floods go down again. The pilgrims must be away before the breaking up of the ice.

Where ?
Who knows ?
Anywhere.

The People Who Run

We had the good fortune to meet the Head Inspector of Refugees in Nijni. He was just starting on a visit of inspection into the country, and very kindly allowed us to accompany him. We travelled in a *troika*, which is the most delightful method of travelling in the world. A troika is an unusually large sleigh drawn by three horses abreast. It is the old-fashioned travelling conveyance and is very seldom seen now in the towns, as, being so wide, it would take up too much room in the street. Ours was a very picturesque, gaily painted troika ; the harness was silver, the reins bright blue, the horses strong spirited animals, who were champing their bits and impatiently pawing at the snow. We got in, burrowed our feet well into a bundle of hay on the floor of the sleigh, were warmly tucked in with a bearskin rug, and were off. We went quietly till we were out of the town, and then the horses began galloping over the trackless snow.

Along the side of the frozen, mighty Volga for a time, and then we turned inland, stopping every now and then at a village or hamlet to inspect the refugees who had been boarded out there. All the villages looked alike, with

140

a large whitewashed church with bright blue or green roofs and domes in the centre, surrounded by a cluster of peasants' cottages. Outside the cottage is generally a cow-shed and a large woodstack. The Russian cottage, or *izba*, is a one-roomed hut. It is built of logs, and the interstices are tightly stuffed with tow to keep out the cold. There is always a large stove, either tiled or of brick, and generally this has a flat top, where the aged members of the family who feel the cold can sleep. A wooden bench runs all along the side of the room, and the other occupants generally sleep either on this or in the big bed, with the homespun linen sheets and coarse embroidered pillow-cases, that fills up most of the room. A picture of the Tsar almost invariably hangs on the wall; in one or two I saw a large picture of our own King shaking hands with him. There is always an eikon hanging in the corner of the room—a perpetual reminder that there is another and a happier world beyond this. Every morning the peasant and his family will stand before the eikon, cross himself and prostrate himself as he says his prayers. In one hut we visited there was a wonderful collection of old eikons in the most pronounced Byzantine style, a black Madonna with a gilt halo and long tapering fingers, Vladimir, Nicholas, and many others that I did not recognize. This woman had also a great array of gilt lamps and candles burning in front of these.

The refugees who are boarded out in these village homes are, of course, treated as members of the family, and take their places on the wooden bench, share the coarse fare of cabbage soup and black bread for daily use, and tea and meat as an occasional luxury. They are naturally expected to share in the indoor or outdoor work of the house. Some of them are rather miserable and home-sick, hating the unaccustomed food, the more extreme cold, and knowing very little of the language. Others, used to a country life, seem to have settled down more or less, and look happy enough. The children go to the village school with the others. Most of the refugees we came across in this district came from Grodno. One woman, a certain Anna Panotocheek, told us her story. These are her own words :

" I have two children—Antonina, who is five, and Gregory, who is two. We had to leave our village in the government of Grodno by command of the Cossacks. My husband had gone to dig trenches, so we left everything behind, I not being able to carry anything besides the children. At times people used to help me carry them, but almost all the way I had to carry one or other of them myself. It was very difficult because they were so heavy. At times I wanted to leave them behind on the roadside. At last we reached a Red Cross station ; there a Sister of Mercy and some officers fed us and warmed us and gave me a rouble. I left in the train for Stonin and from there to Baranovitchi, where I found my husband. We stayed there for several days and then the Germans began throwing bombs, so some one told us it was better to go to Minsk. From there the officials put us in the train for Kazan. Food was provided for us at the Pitatelny Punkt, but some days we received nothing. From home I only brought two skirts and a pair of boots. The soldiers and Cossacks we met on the way were very kind. Then we came here."

One of the very interesting places that we visited on this little tour was the Pechsky Monastery, near Nijni Novgorod. A vene-

143

rable priest met us at the door, blue-gowned, with long white curly hair, and took us round the monastery. Here seventeen refugee clergy families are being housed and looked after—ninety-four people in all. Each family has a fair-sized room to themselves. In some cases the priest has accompanied his family, in other cases he has remained behind. This beautiful old monastery must be a real haven of refuge to these storm-tossed people. The whole place breathes an atmosphere of utter peace.

Before leaving we stood for a few minutes in the beautiful monastery chapel. The walls were glowing with Byzantine eikons, faded rose-crimson, blue, old gold, and these colours were reflected in the dancing lights of the candles burning before each shrine. There was no other illumination in the church, and the corners and the space between the columns was dark with formless shadows. Before the altar a priest, richly vested, was chanting one of the plaintive Slav refrains. The chant was responded to by a blind monk in a black cassock with a wonderful voice. He belonged to one of the contemplative orders, and had been here at this monastery for many years.

144

The thin, reedy voice of the old priest and the rich, deep bass of the monk who responded made a curious echoing cadence that rose and fell rhythmically. There were no seats in the church, and a little group of peasants stood reverently praying before one of the shrines. Then the little boy was lifted up to kiss the eikon of St. Nicholas, patron of sailors and children. And we left them all praying there in the shadows and went on our way.

IX

JEWISH REFUGEES

I HAVE purposely left the chapter on the Jewish refugees to the last, because it is the most difficult to write. It would take a lifetime to really understand the difficulties of the Jewish question in Russia, and it would be sheer impertinence for one who has only been a few months in the country to give any opinion on it. And yet there are so many Jewish refugees that some account of them cannot be omitted, and perhaps it is in some ways easier for a stranger to understand, at least superficially, the very divergent points of view of the Russian and the Hebrew than for one more intimate, who must needs take one side or the other.

Every one who has been to Russia remarks that this is a country of paradoxes, but because it is a platitude, it is none the less true. The reason is that Russia does not

146

advance on the way to civilization by a series of imperceptible gradations, as we older nations do, but rather by dramatic leaps forward. Then, naturally enough, these are followed by periods of reaction. Thus the prohibition of vodka " for ever," which no other nation has been able to accomplish, the Proclamation to Poland, the removal of the disabilities of the Jews, showed the whole world that a new era had dawned for Russia ; yet, at the same time, knowing the history of Russia, one cannot but expect set-backs and cross-currents even in these directions.

The Russian is a *laissez-faire*, genial person, with very little sense of time, and yet Russia is one of the most bureaucratic countries in the world, where everything is wound round and round with red tape from which it is very difficult to extricate oneself. He is a creature of impulse, yet nothing here can be done on the spur of the moment ; one has to wait days sometimes to get a ticket between Petrograd and Moscow, for instance. He has one of the kindest hearts in the world, and yet none can be more intolerant on occasion. He is one of the most trusting of people, yet rooted right down in the Russian heart is a deep distrust of the Jews. It is not without some foundation, for he has suffered much at their hands. The Jew has all the qualities that the Russian has not, and he will fight him on his own ground and win every time. The Russian is lavish, good-natured, and often lazy ; the Jew is prudent, economical, hard-working, far-seeing, and therefore whole villages are sometimes in debt to the Jew. If the harvest happens to be good, the peasant can pay the interest due ; if it is bad he must pledge the next ; and so it goes on from bad to worse. This happens in all grades of society. It is not only the peasants who borrow from the Jew, but the young officer in a crack regiment with a small allowance, the landowner who cannot make both ends meet, the smart Society woman who has card debts she cannot pay. It is the despising of the Jew and yet being beholden to him that has caused a racial dislike in all classes of society, and which has led to the persecution of the Jews, which almost all educated Russians deplore from the bottom of their hearts.

When war broke out, both sides joined hands and tried to forget the past. The Jews realized that Russia was their fatherland and behaved splendidly. A quarter of a million Jews volunteered for military service and fought very bravely, gave large sums of money to the war funds, and did everything possible to prove their loyalty. The Russians, on their side, greatly appreciated the patriotism of the Jews, and ukases were issued removing many of the restrictions and disabilities that had existed before and practically admitting them to the full citizenship of the Russian Empire. The outbreak of war seemed to be the psychological moment when the two races might for the first time begin to understand one another, but after the first acknowledgment of brotherhood a certain reaction took place. It is not possible in one brief moment to break down barriers which have lasted centuries. The Jews have been of all nations and no nation, and their isolation has not been altogether a matter of tragedy for them. They have preferred to live in exile, suffering persecution meekly, knowing that they are the Chosen People, and content to wait patiently for the coming of the Messiah, when the dark ages shall be over and their cause triumphant.

The People Who Run

One of the great difficulties between Russians and Jews since the outbreak of the war has been this: many Jews living near the Russo-German frontier have no special allegiance to either country, and while nominally Russian subjects, have on the whole German sympathies. An enormous amount of spying and underground work has been going on, and this has naturally exasperated the Russians, and particularly the army. Murmurs have been going up on all sides, "Our country is being sold by these horrible Jews." The Jews living near the frontier are for the most part abjectly and sordidly poor, and the prices paid by the Germans for any piece of information useful to them is very high. When one's wife and one's children are near starvation the values of things are apt to change, and many, many succumbed to the temptation and betrayed Russia over and over again. Before the evacuation of Lodz, where there are an enormous number of Jews living, I saw a spy taken red-handed in the act of signalling. He was a typical Polish Jew of the most unprepossessing type, with his side-curls, black skull-cap, and greasy caftan. His face was of a sickly greenish pallor, and he was trembling all over, weeping and begging for mercy. One execrated this man who had betrayed his country in this way, and yet when one saw his wife and children clinging to him and mingling their tears with his, wan and haggard from want of food, one could at least understand his motive.

Russians do not always make a distinction between the traitor Jew, who does not care enough about any country to be loyal to it, and the other kind of Jew whom one meets all over Russia—loyal Russian subjects and keen patriots, self-sacrificing and generous, deploring with all their hearts the treachery of their co-religionists, and yet powerless to help it. One can only dimly guess what a spiritual tragedy this war must be for them.

The language in many cases has given rise to misunderstanding. Yiddish is a kind of bastard German with a mingling of Hebrew phrases. It is universally spoken all over the Russian Pale of Settlement, but it is by no means the case that the Jews speaking it have necessarily German sympathies—only that many of them know no other language.

With all these damning facts against them,

151

it is small wonder that the Jewish refugees living near the frontier had a worse time than any one else at the time of the great flight. Universally suspected of being either spies or at least in sympathy with the Germans, there is no doubt that many individual cases of hardship, injustice, and even cruelty occurred. In the turmoil of the big rush, when everybody was in too much hurry to notice unlawful acts, there were many who had the chance of paying out a private grudge against the Jews, and the latter had no redress, as much of the ill-treatment was winked at by the officials. Their belongings were confiscated, their money taken from them, and whoever else got fed, it was always the Jew who could go without. They suffered from disabilities which other refugees had not to undergo. There are cities where no Jew is allowed to stay, and they are hunted on from pillar to post until at last they find an abiding-place somewhere.

It is only human nature after all, and a helpless, terrified mob of people, fleeing for their lives, cannot be held entirely responsible for their actions. We should probably behave in exactly the same way to people whom we believed were betraying England; but, at

152

the same time, the treatment their poorer brothers received rankled very much in the minds of the patriotic and loyal Jews.

Perhaps there are certain compensations for their hardships. The Jewish refugees do not suffer so acutely from the terrible home-sickness that attacks the refugees of other countries ; they are wanderers by nature or sub-conscious instinct, and are not so rooted to one particular soil as those with a keener sense of nationality. Thus they settle down more quickly than the other refugees and take more easily to new work. Another compensation for them is the extraordinary generosity shown by Jews to their co-religionists. It is a religious duty which none of them ignore, and the money, time, organization, and care given by the Jewish committees to their own people is a model to us all. Of course the Tatiana and other big funds are non-sectarian and give to Jews and Gentiles alike.

Before the war the Russian Pale of Settlement contained about six million Jews. The Pale stretched from the Baltic to the Black Sea, and comprised the ten provinces of Poland, fifteen provinces of Lithuania, part of White Russia, and South-West or Little

153

Russia. About 94 per cent. of all the Jews in Russia lived within the Pale ; those living outside it were chiefly rich merchants, doctors, dentists, and first-class artisans, who received a special permit. It is therefore obvious that a large proportion of the whole number of refugees are Jews, and though many of the disabilities have been removed, there are still some restrictions ; for instance, they may not remain in Petrograd and certain other cities more than seven days without a special permit, which is not very readily granted. The Jewish refugees have mostly been sent far into the interior, and even into Siberia.

Kazan is a typical town in the interior where about a thousand Jewish refugees are living and where their committee is very well managed. Here the Jewish refugees all live in tenement-houses together, so that their food may be kosher, and the religious ceremonies on Sabbaths and festivals duly observed.

Every kind of small trade is represented : jewellers, tailors, pedlars, hawkers, kosher butchers, and dairymen, many of whom can continue their occupation here. They all have the appearance of being town-dwellers : the men with narrow chests and pallid faces ;

the girls, often beautiful, with liquid dark eyes
and raven hair, rather exuberant sometimes,
and more fashionably dressed than any other
refugees we saw, with low-necked blouses and
fancy ear-rings.

These houses are miniature worlds. There
you will find the decent, self-respecting family,
next door the squalid and unclean. The
Polish Jew is notoriously dirty, the Lett just
the reverse, and as they live in very close
quarters indeed, the result must be unpleasant
for the orderly family.

One interesting charity which the Jewish
Committee has arranged at Kazan is a home
for aged refugees. The house is clean, but it
is a rather chilling cleanliness. It is a drab,
dingy, depressing place, and the absence of
children or young people seems to make it
rather dreary, but possibly the old folk are
glad to get away from the noise and turmoil
of the children in the barak. The cooking is
done for them in a special kitchen where all
the ritual connected with the preparation of
the food can be carefully carried out. Other-
wise they do all the work of their own rooms
themselves. The inmates looked exactly as
if they had walked out of the Old Testament.

The People Who Run

There were several old men, with long unshaven beards, engaged in reading the law or the Talmud, arrayed in *talith* or praying-shawl, with phylacteries bound round their foreheads, and round, flat fur caps on their heads. A large square room served them as sitting-room, dining-room, and synagogue. The *mezuzah*, or little wooden case containing the Commandments written on parchment, was set in the lintel of the door, and every pious Jew touches or kisses this every time he passes in. At the farther end of the room was a curtain, screening the wooden Ark of the Covenant, containing two parchment scrolls of the Law, beautifully handwritten in Hebrew characters. The great seven-branched candle-sticks stood on a table ready to be lighted on the Sabbath.

The inmates of this home had been toilers all their lives, and now there was very little for them to do but to give themselves up entirely to the minutiæ of their religion. Each day has its cycle of religious duties—the morning prayers and the ceremonial washing, the recitation of the Law, the Sabbath punc-tuating the week with its special prayers and ceremonies ; and then, as the weeks slide into

156

months, only the yearly festivals will mark the slow progress of the year—the Passover and Pentecost, the New Year, the Great White Fast, the Feast of Tabernacles, and so on to Passover again.

The children have not been forgotten. There were a good many Jewish residents in Kazan before the war, and a Jewish school was started some years ago. Now the refugee children as well as the ordinary resident may attend, and four or five hundred children assemble every day. The little refugees have their midday meal at the school, and we watched them enjoying *tcholent*, a special Jewish dish made of stewed meat with potatoes and beans. At the time of our visit a Hebrew lesson was going on, and a very small, preternaturally wise Jewish boy, whose head just reached to the bottom of the blackboard, was laboriously writing the difficult Hebrew script. The Jewish Refugee Committee has its headquarters at this school, and here the weekly money is doled out, warm clothing given out when required, and an employment bureau is open to all who can work. The rooms are a centre for all the Jewish activities of the district and act as a kind of club for the workers.

157

The People Who Run

To keep their organization going, the Jewish Committee receives a grant from the Government and also from the Tatiana Committee, but they wisely leave the spending of it entirely to the Jewish Committee. Those who can work have, of course, no allowance, but free lodgings are provided for all the refugees.

In the Government of Kazan there are more than two thousand scattered Jews, and their welfare is looked after by their own committee and the Zemsky Cyooz, or County Association, which looks after the scattered country districts. To Tchestipol, a village on the Volga, a whole colony of Ruthenian Jews from Galicia have been sent. The Ruthenians are Slavs by birth, though Austrian subjects, and when the Russians first advanced into Galicia the peasants received them with enthusiasm. When the Russians had to retire these people fled with them, fearing reprisals at the hands of the Austrians. At the same time, a large number of the Ruthenian Jews were sent under arrest to Kiev, on suspicion that they might give information to the enemy on their return. These were sent on as far as possible into the interior, and they suffered a great deal before they were finally established. They were hardly refugees in the ordinary sense of the word, as they were under police or military supervision, but they were almost more to be pitied than any of the fugitives. Ignorant, bewildered, many of them were of the lowest class, with dirty, insanitary habits that brought serious epidemics with them, and very few of them knowing a word of Russian.

Very sad cases of distress come before the Jewish Committee from time to time. There was a family in Kazan, living in one little room, who had been extremely wealthy and had lost everything they had. They had been living in Poland and had been ordered by the military authorities to quit the town at once as the Germans were rapidly advancing. They managed to lay their hands on three thousand roubles, and as they possessed two large barges, they decided to sail down the river to Kiev, bringing as much furniture with them as the barges would carry. But a Jewish festival was due just then, and they foolishly decided to wait till it was over. The Russian military authorities, finding they had

not started when they were told to, got hold
of the idea that they had German sympathies
and were waiting till the German troops
entered the town to give them information.
Their barges and money were confiscated and
they were turned penniless out of the town,
and are now living in miserable poverty in
Kazan. But in spite of unfortunate incidents
like this, which must occur during any war,
a new respect between the Russians and the
Jews is steadily growing, and it is hoped that
the old prejudices will disappear. The heroic
action of one young Jewish medical student
at the front has done a very great deal to raise
the status of Jews throughout the whole of
Russia. In the middle of a fierce battle near
Goldap, the Russian standard-bearer was
bayoneted by a German soldier and the flag
captured. Young Osnas, a Jewish medical
student from Vilna, seeing his chance, sprang
forward, killed the German soldier and seized
the flag, though he was entirely surrounded
for a few moments by the enemy striving to
recapture it once more. Osnas, although
severely wounded, managed to hold it until
reinforcements came up. For the heroic

courage he showed the Emperor himself decorated him with the St. George's Cross, the highest reward for courage a Russian soldier can obtain. May it be a happy omen for the future.

X

CONCLUSION

THE estimated number of refugees in Russia
varies a good deal. Different officials have
given numbers varying from 3,000,000 to
6,500,000 in round figures. The difficulty in
getting an accurate estimate has been very
great—first, because the districts have not all
sent in their returns as yet; secondly, the
estimated number of refugees means the
total number of people who have applied
for Government assistance, and not the
total number of those who have fled. In
the large cities—Moscow, Petrograd, and
Kiev—there are numbers of refugees being
registered every day. This was difficult
to understand at first as the Germans
have hardly advanced anywhere since the
autumn of 1915, and in some places they
have been pushed back. On inquiry one
found that some of these were refugees

Conclusion

who had been living in the woods as near
to their old home as possible, hoping for
an opportunity to return. The unusually
severe winter and difficulty of getting food
drove these refugees into the interior and
large towns. But the majority of the
newly registered refugees were people who
had fled and had been living in the towns
for some time on their small savings. These
having been quite exhausted, they were
obliged in the end to register themselves
as refugees. One of the most complete
lists gives the total number of registered
refugees in Russia on January 1, 1916, as
3,241,983. The actual number of fugitives is probably nearer 5,000,000, for
the reasons given above. That is to say
that in addition to her enormous war
task, Russia is looking after and main-
taining more refugees than there are people
in the whole of the continent of Australia.
It seems a burden almost greater than any
country could bear, but Russia can bear it,
and even more if it were necessary. Russia
has not yet become alive to her own immense
resources, she has allowed unscrupulous

foreigners to exploit her too long, but there are signs that she is awaking from her long sleep. Any help that can be given her now will be repaid a thousand-fold in the day when Russia shall realize her mighty heritage.

Appendix

Refugees in Russia
January 1
1916

Russia in Europe
Under the County Association

Astrakhan Government		.	.	20,400
Bessarabia	,,	.	.	3,560
Vitebsk	,,	.	.	52,938
Vladimir	,,	.	.	23,955
Vologda	,,	.	.	13,077
Volensk	,,	.	.	87,347
Voronej	,,	.	.	47,000
Viatka	,,	.	.	2,944
Ekaterinoslav	,,	.	.	317,633
Kazan	,,	.	.	51,667
Kalonga	,,	.	.	64,780
Kiev	,,	.	.	30,097
Kostroma	,,	.	.	10,729
Kursk	,,	.	.	78,895
Minsk	,,	.	.	116,812
Mogilef	,,	.	.	73,773
Moscow	,,	.	.	173,257
City of Moscow	.	.	.	140,107
Nijni Novgorod	,,		.	58,157
Novgorod	,,		.	18,041
	Forward			1,385,169

Appendix

Brought Forward				1,385,169
Olonetz Government			.	337
Orenburg ,,			.	64,844
Orel ,,			.	36,033
Pensa ,,			.	62,903
Perm ,,			.	24,923
Petrograd ,,				list not complete
City of Petrograd	.	.	.	84,074
Town of Kronstadt	.	.	.	473
Poltava Government	.	.	.	29,106
Pskoff ,,	.	.	.	18,706
Podolsk ,,	.	.	.	5,474
Riazan ,,	.	.	.	68,184
Samara ,,	.	.	.	136,646
Saratof ,,	.	.	.	108,617
Simbirsk ,,	.	.	.	39,687
Smolensk ,,	.	.	.	42,286
Stavropol ,,	.	.	.	6,271
Tavrida	.	.	.	39,574
Sebastopol Town .	.	.	.	315
Kerch	.	.	.	752
Tambov Government	.	.	.	127,281
Tver ,,	.	.	.	31,606
Tula ,,	.	.	.	37,404
Ufa ,,	.	.	.	70,085
Harkovsk ,,	.	.	.	116,797
Town of Harkovsk	.	.	.	42,150
Kherson Government	.	.	.	39,118
Odessa, City of	.	.	.	13,680
Tchernikof .	.	.	.	35,346
Yaroslav	.	.	.	33,406

2,701,247

Appendix

RUSSIA IN EUROPE (*Cont.*)

Not under County Association

Archangel Government . .	2,109
Colonies on the Don . . .	73,594
Rostoff	13,241
Livonia	list not complete
Esthonia	7,585
	96,529

Caucasus

Baku	4,600
Elisabetpol	10,238
Tiflis	7,390
Tchernomorsk	2,541
Erivan	105,030
Batum	12,000
Dagestan	299
Kars	17,189
Kuban	12,120
Tersk	2,257
Soochmeesky	42
	173,706

Asiatic Russia

(*a*) Yeniseisk Government . .	1,981
Irkutsk ,, . .	8,616
Baikalia ,, . .	2,800
Yakutsk ,, .	list not complete
Amur Region . . .	1,958
Forward	15,355

Appendix

ASIATIC RUSSIA (*Cont.*)

Brought Forward			15,355	
Premorsk	.	.	.	.	2,547	
Town of Vladivostok	.	.	1,627	
				19,529

(b) Akmolinsk	.	.	.	.	29,871	
Semipalatinsk	.	.	.	576	
				30,447
				49,976

(c) *Turkestan :*

Caspian Regions	.	.	.	13,846
Samarkand	.	.	.	12,900
Semirechensk	.	.	.	11,252
Siv Daria	.	.	.	24,328
Ferghan	.	.	.	20,695
				83,021

(d) *Siberia :*

Tobolsk	.	.	.	16,091
Tomsk	.	.	.	38,445
Turgai	.	.	.	16,721
Ural Regions	.	.	.	6,467
				77,724

(c) Tarnopol	.	.	.	2,700
Bokhara	.	.	.	800
Chita	.	.	.	680
Vansk	.	.	.	6,000
Bajazet	.	.	.	1,000
Diadinsk	.	.	.	8,600
Hopsk	.	.	.	5,000
Forward			24,780

Appendix

ASIATIC RUSSIA (*Cont.*)

	Brought Forward	24,780	
Dilmansk	. . . .	25,000	
Urm	. . . .	10,000	
		———	59,780
Total	. . . .		270,501

Total European Russia	. .	2,971,482
„ Asiatic „	. .	270,501
Grand total	. . . .	3,241,983

Index

173

Index

174

Index

Index

Help the Homeless People of Poland

BY CONTRIBUTING TO THE

Great Britain to Poland Fund

(with which is affiliated the British Moscow Relief Committee)

N.B.—No contributions pass through German or Austrian hands. The money collected is sent to the Russo-Asiatic Bank in Petrograd, and considerable profit is made on the extremely favourable rate of exchange. In normal times Russia gives us 95 roubles for £10, but at present she gives us 150 roubles for £10. The English equivalent of a rouble is a fraction over 2s. 1d.

Twenty Shillings will keep Twenty People from Starvation for a Week

COMMITTEES HAVE BEEN ESTABLISHED IN ALL THE PRINCIPAL CITIES OF THE UNITED KINGDOM

Patrons :
THE ARCHBISHOP OF CANTERBURY. THE EARL OF ROSEBERY.
HIS EXCELLENCY SIR C. W. BUCHANAN,
British Ambassador Extraordinary and Plenipotentiary at Petrograd.

Chairman : THE LADY BYRON.

Hon. Secretary : C. W. NICHOLSON, Esq.

Hon. President : THE LORD MAYOR OF LONDON.

Hon. Vice-Presidents :
THE DUKE OF NEWCASTLE. SIR HORACE PLUNKETT.
THE VISCOUNT BRYCE. SIR FREDERICK POLLOCK, Bart.
The Ven. ARCHDEACON CUNNINGHAM.

Hon. President Edinburgh Committee :
THE LORD DUNEDIN.

Hon. President Glasgow Committee :
THE LORD PROVOST OF GLASGOW.

Hon. President Manchester Committee :
THE LORD MAYOR OF MANCHESTER.

Patrons, Liverpool Committee :
THE LORD MAYOR OF LIVERPOOL. THE EARL OF DERBY.

Hon. Treasurer :
EVELEIGH NASH, Esq.,
36 King Street, Covent Garden, LONDON.

Auditors : LEONARD G. LANE AND Co., 56 Ludgate Hill, E.C.
Bankers : THE RUSSO-ASIATIC BANK, 6 Old Broad Street, E.C.
Cheques and Postal Orders should be made payable to " Great Britain to Poland Fund."

CPSIA information can be obtained at www.ICGtesting.com
Printed in the USA
BVOW04s0527300115

385680BV00018B/135/P